PRODUCT TEAM COACH

VALUE & OUTCOME-DRIVEN SOLUTIONS FOR TURNING IDEAS INTO PRODUCTS

JORDAN COLLIER

Copyright 2022, by Jordan Collier
ISBN: 978-0-578-37236-5

Content Editors: Phil Collier, Joshua Collier, Clint Hill,
Matt Eland, Shayleen Smith
Grammatical Editors: Shayleen Smith, Mrs. Gugeler aka "Mama G"
Cover and Book Design: Lindsey Baker Allred
Illustrations: Isaac Collier (Years of Minute-To-Pen-It have led to this.)

Published by:
Jordan Collier
Spring Hill, Tennessee
productteamcoach.com
jordanicollier.com

Table of Contents

A Message From the Author

The first time I helped shape and lead an idea which eventually turned into something that actually saved people's lives when it was implemented, I knew I was hooked on productization and how to make it more accessible. Knowing that others' lives were dependent on how I ensured the product team was communicating in unison with each other made me realize there were times when there were too much tribal knowledge, opinions or barriers-to-entry to actually get started on delivering something of value that I wanted to create a starting point for members of a product team or the product persons themselves.

If you are reading this as part of a preview or have stumbled upon it one way or another and are unable to afford it in your current season, contact me. Together, we can work something out to ensure you can get this resource in your hands.

If you have any questions or feedback, please reach out to me at jordanicollier@gmail.com.

Preface

The intention, desire, and hope in writing the following pages is to assist you in breaking down your barriers to understand what creating and running a product entails. What makes this book unique is that it is purposefully crafted not to ascribe to any one style of Agile or iterative delivery of work, but instead focuses on the outcomes of team collaboration. Let this book help you enter into a clearer understanding of how to turn ideas into living, breathing products.

There are three potential readers who can benefit from this book:

1. People who are completely new or curious about the field of product management, ownership, or leadership.

2. People who are already in the field but want additional understanding and direction for their team and product.

3. Leaders who want to integrate running their ideas or work like a product so they can learn from their findings and iterate as needed.

It does not matter whether you are an entrepreneur, software engineer, product person, executive, dolphin trainer, entertainer, or in fast food, you will be able to apply these principles in some fashion. Take the parts from this book which work best for you, though a good starting place would be to incorporate it all, and then iterate as needed. The content in this book has been proven to work together cohesively.

This book is meant to be read from front to back, and be utilized as a referenceable guide. There are so many organizations, schools, certifications, and companies out in the world vying for your attention and money. This in turn can cause confusion as to where to find information or even where to start the journey towards understanding what it means to actually care for a product or how even to create one.

So what is the singular/primary reason for you to read this book? Your current frustrations or ideas. This book is for you. Someone eagerly seeking to understand how to run a product, realizing that it is so easy to get misdirected. For you, the seeker, this book is intended to help you avoid following pointless rabbit trails which could be outdated or cost more time than you are planning on allocating just for being curious.

FLOW OF THE BOOK

This book will first go over what it means to be a Product Team Coach (PTC). In some industries this role is referred to as a Product Manager or Product Owner, however it can be so much more, so it will be referred to as the PTC from this point forward.

After that, you will learn how to identify the members of your team called the Product Team Members. With the Product Team Members you will then learn to turn ideas new or old into a product (Productization) which should be worked on or even avoided based on the value collectively established. Once productization is discussed, there will be a section on how to lead Product Team Members daily/weekly using outcome-driven ceremonies. There is a small section with how to break into the industry if you are not yet in it. Finally, there is a worksheet resource with examples and an additional guide to help inspire conversations you can reference when leading these outcome-driven approaches during your Scoping sessions.

The intention, desire, and hope in writing *Product Team Coach*, is to help you enter into a clearer understanding of how to turn ideas into living/breathing products.

A NOTE FROM THE AUTHOR: Some concepts in this book may be unfamiliar. Rather than simplifying each of them, you are encouraged to explore these concepts from their original source. For any terms you are unfamiliar with there is also a glossary that has been put together in the back of this book.

Who is Jordan Collier?

Jordan Collier currently is a product specialist helping companies and individuals turn their ideas into products globally. This knowledge which has been sought after through conventional and unconventional sources has sparked a journey working as a software engineer turned Product Team Coach (PTC). He has helped form, design, set-up, and create product labs across multiple Fortune 100 companies, some of which were in the top 5.

He has also helped create internal bootcamps which train individuals how to be a product team member and PTC and began standardizing the way a business communicates products across teams and users. He has also helped create internal bootcamps which train individuals how to be a product team member and PTC and began standardizing the way a business communicates products across teams and users.

Jordan is passionate about this line of work and hopes this resource helps you find clarity as you seek greater understanding within this discipline.

PART I

Product Team

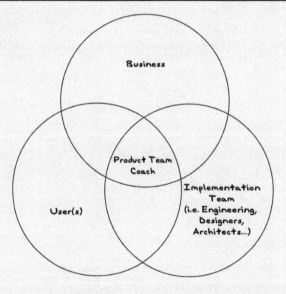

Product Team Members

Business

Product Team Coach

User(s)

Implementation Team (i.e. Engineering, Designers, Architects...)

1

Product Team Coach and Product Team Members

Product Team Coaches (PTC) are at the center of a team's communication and interaction. They take ideas new and old from involved parties related to the product which they can extract information from. This is to ensure that when the idea is implemented that it is valued and understood. The PTC is the catalyst which leads the rest of the team involved to empathy and shared understanding. To provide further detail, imagine a team as a Venn Diagram, like the one found above. The Product Team Members would be the makeup of all of these circles together, which would include design, stakeholders, the PTC, implementers, users and more as you see fit.

EMPATHY

In order for you to be a top-tier PTC, you must be an advocate of empathy. Each Product Team Member involved has a different perspective and need, and can offer a wide range of information as it relates to a product. The PTC must learn to understand the language of each of the Product Team Members involved. The PTC needs to be attentive to the team's pain points, to whom teams report, what is tied to each of the Product Team Members' impact or the lack of the product existing. When offered a problem, each of the Product Team Members will have a different solution, or may view a problem differently. This is where the PTC comes in. The PTC's responsibility is not just to understand the Product Team Members situation, job description, and responsibilities, but to coach them all collaboratively on a journey towards empathy and shared understanding.

SHARED UNDERSTANDING

Miscommunication can threaten the integrity of a team. To mitigate this, it's important to recognize that questions lead to conversation, conversation leads to connection, and connection leads to a stronger community. When these steps are taken, the team can properly have a shared understanding of what is happening.

It is the PTC's job to guide conversations and translate what each Product Team Member wants to communicate in a way that is understood consistently. For example, say you are dealing with a highly technical engineer who begins to show you many lines of code, expertly crafted yielding a solution to be implemented. If those you need to communicate with are not technical, then you need to find a way to best show or advocate the implementation without losing them with all of the technical speak. You want to constantly find opportunities to equip each Product Team Member with relevant information that will help communicate the product's initiatives in a way that many people can understand, regardless of their technical background. Regardless of technical speak, it is often the simple things which trip people up, and all that is needed is an outcome driven conversation.

This is a commonly used illustration which displays what it means to have shared understanding as you begin your product journey. Imagine you pull in Product Team Members similar to the picture above and present them with a problem that needs a solution by saying, "Let's solve the issue of trying to commute in the city by utilizing a means of transportation with only two wheels." Then you dismiss the team, without further collaboration, each member could leave the room working on their own solution for a two-wheeled vehicle but are unknowingly misaligned based on their way of seeing the problem in their world. One person could bring back the solution for a motorcycle, and another would bring back their idea for a wheel in each of your shoes. Let's say that in reality, all that was needed was a simple scooter. Each one of those solutions addresses different problems, but all that needed to happen was a conversation that fosters shared understanding of the main goal. The PTC can help in this situation. The PTC needs to confirm not just a shared understanding among all the Product Team Members, but needs to ensure shared collaboration as well.

You might think this is straightforward, but if the PTC were not involved, that conversation simply would not have happened at all or it would have happened with a strong background bias influencing each individual. One of the responsibilities of the PTC is to check that all inevitable irrelevant bias and miscommunication is eliminated to ensure efficient coaching for all team members.

When team members wait for conversations to happen naturally, they are setting themselves up for many headaches and potentially the failure of a product. The PTC is the conversation initiator. Every single thing a PTC does should be based on a conversation. The PTC is ensuring consistency of thoughts, alignment, and direction among the team. Anytime the Product Team Members leave the PTC out of the conversation, a product's demise or defeat begins knocking on the door.

DON'T WORK OFF OF ASSUMPTIONS

Throughout the rest of this book, you may notice a pattern: have focused conversations, ensure shared understanding, exemplify empathy, and lead with an outcome. This pattern can quickly lose its effectiveness if assumptions are not addressed. Assumptions lead to misinformation which can quickly become a poison that causes misunderstanding within the team. If misunderstanding makes its rounds, the community is suddenly threatened and the hope of connection is lost. Remember, questions lead to conversations which lead to connection, which lead to community and teamwork. These lead to the final goal of shared understanding.

UNDERSTANDING THE MAKEUP OF THE PRODUCT TEAM MEMBERS

It is important to remember that as a PTC, you're working with people. Naturally, people tend to bring what they care about into all aspects of their lives, including their work with any product. Because of this, all who are involved in the life cycle of the product will want to know more about what it is they can offer/take from the product. For instance:

- Stakeholders might be more interested in what a product means for their business, or how to effectively communicate progress to their peers from a higher level perspective.

- The user may want to know when they can begin to benefit from the product or when they can start utilizing the product.

- The PTC may be more interested in ensuring the product is not becoming bloated and has a clear direction. Most importantly, as the person running the outcome driven initiatives in this book, the PTC is constantly looking and feeling the dynamics of the people in any engagements. The PTC is ensuring things are not just said and lost but instead written down for reference, and that the right people are always in the room talking.

THE PTC'S COLLABORATION WITH THE BUSINESS

Simply put, a business is seeking a certain value and is funding the product. The business stakeholders or owners are the ones who should want to know whether the product being built is worth their time and money. If the business stakeholder or owner is not actively involved in the findings, discovery, progress, and updates, the benefit of what the PTC and Product Team Members offer will feel like a waste or as if they are not contributing any value.

The PTC must over-communicate. The PTC must over communicate and keep the owner or stakeholder involved and show the value of the product outcomes and initiatives. The PTC also must communicate to keep the Product Team Members fully engaged.

At the same time the Stakeholders/owners cannot solely call the shots because they have the checkbook. While some may try to do this, the PTC should be looking for a business that empowers you as the PTC, to make the calls and see whether something is of value or not. If you, as the PTC, are not empowered to make decisions and talk to the people you need to, due to title or having to navigate through a hierarchy of people, communicating effectively quickly loses its feasibility. Responsibility and trust must be given and received by the PTC. Just imagine if college sports coaches had to navigate through a hierarchy of people each time they called a play. A single game would take years to play and opportunity would be lost.

IMPLEMENTATION TEAM

The implementation team is the part of the Product Team Members that quite frankly "gets stuff done." They are the ones that the PTC will spend a lot of time with to help carry out the implementation of the vision for the product. In a technical team the implementation team is not just made up of engineers, but also designers in many cases. The PTC must be a great listener and have a lot of empathy. This area takes the most conscious work because you are dealing with thinkers who are constantly solving problems as it relates to the product implementation you have agreed upon. The PTC must put in the work and earn the trust of these Product Team Members. If you, as the PTC, are leading a product, yet you do not understand any of the implementation they are building out, you can quickly be thrown for a loop and lose product leadership and influence.

AUTHOR'S NOTE: As the PTC you are managing the product not the individuals of the team. Keep this in mind as there are plenty of reasons this can be beneficial and help encourage a desired trust in conversation and collaboration.

COMMONLY ASKED QUESTIONS

What does a day in the life of a PTC look like?

Daily Product Team Coaches will:

- Validate the product's current hypothesis and metrics that reflect what is being done to move the idea for the product forward while ensuring the work is properly organized.

- Attempt to stay ahead of the work currently being implemented. If you are finding you are running out of work to do, there is a chance that you need to have another conversation with the stakeholder and user.

- Be highly available to communicate to and from your fellow Product Team Members, i.e., developers, designers, users, stakeholders, etc.

- If you have designers on the Product Team, constantly meet with them to validate that the design is reflected in the stories.

- Review stories that are ready to be accepted/returned. The faster a completed story moves to a user, the faster you can get feedback.

- Run daily/weekly ceremonies

- Check and validate metrics

- Prepare the next MVP and hypothesis for new products or the current product

What is the difference among a PTC, product owner and a product manager?

Truthfully it depends on the business of the people running a product and their needs. You can find articles from well respected product people in the industry and have many conversations with those who will argue both sides and what they should or should not do with those roles. This book tries to simplify it and "combine" the roles and refer to them as a Product Team Coach. It is not the easy way out, quite honestly, the best way to learn about the difference is to ask that question with each business with which you interact.

Whenever you talk with a business ask these two questions:

1. What is the product owner at your business responsible for?

2. What is the product manager at your business responsible for?

From these 2 questions a lot of characteristics will be shown about whether you would like to lead a product for them or whether you should keep looking. You never know, you might even find their approach is better than anything else you have ever heard about and adopt their methods yourself.

PART II

Productization

Productization is classified by 3 steps that you may go through in this book: Scoping, Discovery and Framing, and Inception. Each will be broken down and explained in greater detail.

2

What is a Product?

Oftentimes when people hear the word "product" they may think of something sold in a store, or something you put in your hair to make it look a certain way. While both of these things can certainly be a product, it is so much more.

A product is any idea, work, or initiative which can be iterated on continuously. How it is discussed and iterated on is up to the Product Team Coach and the involved Product Team Members. This is not a book which is going to prescribe the only way a product can be tackled, rather, this book will suggest an outcome driven path that has worked well for hundreds of thousands of people. It all comes down to conducting conversation and including all those involved in the process to continuously deliver value.

It is time to begin talking about how a PTC takes an idea, or even an existing implementation, and productizes it. Examples in this book will generally default to software, however, this practice can be applied to nearly every idea and implementation, regardless of industry.

PRODUCTS ARE LIVING AND BREATHING

All this means is that the product must be taken care of actively. It is not self-sustaining and if it is left alone, it can die, decompose or worse; it could stink up the entire place. A product must have its vitals cared for. To do this, you must take inventory of its vitals. You can do this by asking questions like:

- How are its vitals (metrics, goals, and hypothesis)?
- Does it still have value which can be derived from it?

- Is it relevant or obsolete?
- Is it too small? Too big?
- Do people know it exists?
- Are the right people interacting with it?

All of the previous questions must be asked on a daily basis. If a product is wasting your time and money, something may need to change. People do not get excited about something that wastes their time, money or smells bad.

PRODUCTIZATION PROCESS

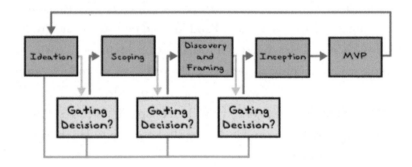

Each one of the steps on the top row represent the coming together of the Product Team Members discussing what direction the potential product should take next. The steps lead to a process called *productization*. Each Scoping session, Discovery and Framing phase, and Inception session has a section in this book dedicated to explaining how to facilitate each with the Product Team Members to ensure shared understanding, shared direction, and aligned expectations.

MVP (MINIMUM VALUABLE PRODUCT)

So you want to learn how to build things people love? Not waste money? Not waste time? It all starts here. It all starts with conversation, prototypes, and measurable experiments in a controlled space. Before digging into the productization methods there is a concept that needs to be covered first which is the MVP (Minimum Valuable Product).

An MVP (Minimum Valuable Product) is the simplest thing you can deliver which brings value in turn to receive valuable feedback. The reason to deliver the MVP is to understand whether you should continue in the direction you are heading or if you should switch directions altogether as quickly as possible. This desired outcome helps cut out the guessing. This way of organizing thoughts, conversation, and direction is centered around this outcome of implementing an MVP. You want to deliver the absolute minimum, to get the absolute maximum from a product. One of the ways industry experts have done so is by utilizing a style called Lean. A resource that helps break this down is Eric Ries's, The Lean Startup. Since the points of Ries' work will help build the framework for productization, below you will find a brief synopsis of his key points. While the following is a quick summary of his documented style, this should never replace the full wisdom contained in his book.

KEY POINTS OF "LEAN"

Eric Ries is a prominent author of the Build-Measure-Learn theory, in The Lean Startup. He discusses a way of obtaining feedback about an idea or product and how to validate its value in the current market. This style of development can reduce risk when delivering a solution and helps you determine whether you are building the right product or not, quickly.

The following steps make up the Build-Measure-Learn feedback loop:

1. **Plan** your hypothesis. You do this through Scoping sessions and the Discovery and Framing phase, both of which will be explained later in great detail.

2. **Build** and deliver an MVP so that you can test it and start collecting feedback.

3. **Measure** using your metrics with the hypothesis created earlier in the plan phase.

4. **Learn** from the metrics, and user feedback, to determine if you need to persevere or pivot. Once you have gone through all 4 steps, you can start at step one again.

PRODUCTIZING

So here it is, the meat and potatoes of the process it takes to take your current work or idea into something you can manage. With each step of the process, it is important to remember a concept that was brought up earlier: all outcomes are driven by conversation. If people are not talking to each other, then the concepts in this book simply fall apart. It's hard to tell a story with others when you don't know much about the characters or setting. You may think that people will naturally talk to each other, but that is quite simply not the case. You have to give all involved a platform to discuss their thoughts, pains, and ideas. A majority of problems can be solved just by talking out loud to each other. Since conversation can make or break an outcome, the next few chapters will be dedicated to building a framework for communication. By following the steps provided in productizing, you will not only be one step closer to having a product, but you will be surrounded with the creation of a valuable resource called shared understanding. People may not talk for a myriad of reasons, but one of the most common reasons is because they simply do not understand or "think" that everyone else understands like they do. The productization process starts from the ground up and constantly ensures everyone involved is synced up. Where there are questions, be sure there are people or processes in place to help find answers. If there is only one thing you get out of this book, let it be this: a PTC should constantly be ensuring and pursuing shared understanding with the entire product team by encouraging conversation.

> **AUTHOR'S NOTE:** Throughout the life of a product, you want to make sure that those with the loudest voices are not the only ones heard. It is crucial to have a PTC who will check in with each person giving each a chance to speak and share their perspective and understanding and not warrant only HiPPOs (or Highest Paid Person's Opinion) to dominate.

Now to your first point of contact with the potential product: the idea.

IDEA

Before you start productizing an idea, make sure it is written down. Make sure the idea makes sense to the PTC. If you are not the one with the idea, make sure those with the idea are in a place where they are ready to start talking about it. Everybody processes ideas in different ways and you want to make sure there is at least one problem tied to the product that is being solved. If there is no problem to solve, there is a chance it may be too soon to tackle or it may not be of significant value to solve. Which ideas to take in or not is entirely subjective, but a good rule of thumb is, "Work on the problem which brings the most value that you are aware of."

WORK IN PROGRESS

If the work is already in progress, then you may experience some healthy growing pains when implementing the practices of this book, which should be expected and beneficial. The advice here is to start with the entire team from the beginning of the process which is called the Scoping session (which will be covered in the next section). The sooner you can get the Product Team Members talking, the better.

Try never to feel as though you have missed the opportunity to run an idea or already existing implementation as a product. You may find that a product you thought was dead needed to pivot to bring forth its value or that what was delivered is providing a lot of unrecognized value. A myriad of results can happen when you start paying attention to the work being delivered.

THE POWER OF SHARED VOCABULARY

Every single word stated and shared from this point on needs to be clearly defined, understood, and agreed upon. If you hear a term being used in different ways, stop the conversation immediately to clear up the conversation. You are doing a soft reset and beginning the creation of a language which everyone should adopt and begin to speak. Speaking the same language extends past your geolocated tongue - it is understanding what terminology to use in relation to a shared direction. This is especially helpful when dealing with a highly technical product and business owners or users who may not be technical. Set the precedent that there is no shame in asking what something means, because not only are you digging deeper into a meaning, but you are helping each Product Team Member begin to speak the same language which carries forth the team's vision.

It's important to note that a shared vocabulary is a great opportunity to exemplify empathy across the Product Team Members. When dealing with people who are not technical in an area, be patient and break down any meanings. If you are in a scenario where people are not willing to break down a meaning, this is a budding sign of something much worse: knowledge silos, fear, secrets, pride or arrogance. Either way, as the PTC, you set the example of what it looks like to patiently communicate with your team in an empathetic way.

DOES ALL OF THIS TAKE PLACE IN PERSON OR REMOTELY?

Many companies faced the challenge of going remote when the global COVID-19 pandemic hit. Because of their adaptability and creativity, most work happened remotely and continues even as this book is being written. The examples in this book will take place as if all work is done in a remote environment, however, they have also been proven to work just as effectively in person.

Using a software space that enables everyone to discuss and interact on the same shared space allows for free movement. Look for software which allows for the creation of digital interactable whiteboards and sticky notes.

HOW OFTEN SHOULD YOU GO THROUGH THE PRODUCTIZATION PROCESS AFTER THE FIRST TIME IT HAS BEEN DONE?

When you find that the hypothesis can be confirmed (successful or failure), have the next hypothesis ready to go. Sometimes you cannot make the next hypothesis until the current one is validated or invalidated. Just be ready to scope out the next bit of work when that happens and go through the productization process again (i.e., Scoping sessions, the Discovery and Framing phase, Inception sessions, and Implementation).

WHEN IS THE PRODUCT DONE?

The product is done when it no longer provides value. Whether it is in its infancy or is of a significant age, there will always be work needed to improve the product. Therefore, the amount of work needed to be done isn't a good gauge of whether or not a product is of any value. Value is not based on how many people are asking for something but rather from the business and product goals that are in scope.

3

Scoping

You have the idea, now it is time for something called Scoping, or a Scoping session. Scoping sessions are scribed conversations that begin to lay the foundation around a potential or existing product led by the PTC and known relevant Product Team Members.

Whether you are running just one product or an entire portfolio of products, it is important that every single one of them has a Scoping session document.

Scoping sessions should occur when:

- An idea is formulated about a problem/solution
- When you have delivered a hypothesis and are ready for the next iteration
- Whenever an existing or potential product is identified
- Work is being done, but it is disorganized

It is never too late to have a Scoping session; you can have a Scoping session on products that are decades old or even on an idea with no software/hardware/system in place. What is most important is that you have a Scoping session. Everybody involved on a team should be able to recite what a Scoping session sought to find out after it was completed. If you find your team is disorganized or there is dissonance in terms of the goal, engaging in a Scoping session can help recalibrate the team. Just remember: when in doubt, Scope it out.

Outcome of a Scoping session:

The goal is to enable shared understanding amongst the Product Team Members regarding a single idea which can be referenced via document throughout the life of the product. Begin to define the potential product, problem to be solved, and why the business should care.

Who:

PTC of the potential product, implementers, designers, stakeholder(s), user*

A user is great to have if enough is known about the product; sometimes more work needs to be done before you can pull them in due to not knowing if they even exist yet.

How long:

Around one hour

Approach and additional resources:

At Appendix B in the back of this book, you will find a Scoping Worksheet with examples that have been put together to use for reference.

DEMYSTIFY WHETHER THE IDEA IS A PROJECT OR PRODUCT

A project may have an end state or a desired result which does not need to be improved upon or continued once implemented. A non-technical example would be like buying land for your farming ventures. Once it is bought, there is not more to do. You have achieved and purchased the plot; it is done.

A product on the other hand, is something that will be delivered, measured, and iterated on. A non-technical example would be the planting of the crops, where you are constantly adapting to the weather, market, and needs to effectively buy and sell your crop based on what you view as the highest value. After a Scoping session is completed, it is not uncommon to realize that what was originally thought to be a product is now a project or vice versa.

Some more examples of a product:	Some more examples of a product:
• Training initiative for all development teams to go through to use the new security software that was just bought by the end of a quarter • Replacing all of the old computers in an office within a certain budget and time	• A music application which allows users to identify artists being played at live events • An automation which enables developers to focus on menial tasks that come up daily, pulling them away from their current work • An application that helps remind vehicle owners how often they need to have general maintenance for their vehicles, based on the distance traveled as shown on the phones' GPS information

HOW TO RUN A SCOPING SESSION

To run this Scoping session, you will go from category to category below filling in the details as a team. You have to make certain that what will be talked about still brings value or is worth solving. There are many times when, after a Scoping session, the potential product may no longer be a problem worth solving.

Facilitating a Scoping session takes time to learn, and the more you are a part of such sessions, the more you can start learning good patterns or signs that may be out-of-scope. Keep with it, and trust that every time you facilitate one of these sessions that you will learn more about your approach and your audience. The more you run, the more you will get a feel of what could be missing from session to session, or what might need further collaboration. Put yourself in a position where you are doing as many of these Scoping sessions as possible. Don't be surprised if it takes 20 sessions to feel confident in how to run them. While you're learning what an effective Scoping session looks and sounds like, keep in mind that it is never meant to produce a highly prescriptive document which restricts new learnings or findings. Its purpose is to encourage shared understanding.

AUTHOR'S NOTE: There is also a completed Scoping session which can be referenced in the back of the book to help inspire your first productization session in this presented style.

3.1

Product Name

While all the aspects of a product are important, the name is what sets the theme for the rest of the Scoping session. The name is the basic foundation to build shared understanding upon. As the PTC, make sure to pick a name that is easy to say, and makes sense to those who may not even be a part of this Scoping session. When everyone leaves the meeting and there are questions about the product, all should be referring to it as the agreed upon name. As the PTC, you may need to weed through people's biases to come to a point of commonality, as earlier discussed. For example, the stakeholder might call the product "the money maker" while the user might call it "the lifesaver". When the name is defined, it is the PTC's responsibility to clearly communicate the name, the reason for the name, and the importance of continuity regarding its name. Once this has been clarified, you can move on to each person's role in the meeting.

3.2

Product Team Members/Requestor

Here you should identify why each person is there in the Scoping session. Call out each role and their expected responsibilities for the time being - the stakeholder, the user, the implementers, the PTC, and anyone else who might be related to solving the problem attached to the potential product. Not only is it important to create a space where everyone gets to know each other, but this is one of the first steps to instill ownership within the team. Make sure that every known aspect of a potential product is owned, understood, and that it is noted on something that can be easily accessed by participants. From this point on, the PTC is the point-person for any questions, concerns or ideas. It is a big responsibility, but the PTC must be the chief communicator. If this step is skipped, expectations and a loss for where to get information can begin. Imagine the PTC as a phone operator who knows the proper numbers to call, the means of connection, and how to connect relevant people who need to work together.

3.3

Value Category (Pick One)

In this section of the Scoping session, the rule of thumb is to pick one of the following categories to help align what value is attached to the solving of the problem. If anyone on the call has a hard time finding the value, make note of that and ask the team, "Is this just an exciting idea or does it actually bring value?"

The subsections that follow will break down each of the most common business categories that a PTC deals with. Though it may be tempting to pick multiple, the suggestion is to try and align the participants to pick only one which is the best fit. What can tend to happen is someone will say, "Oh it is all of them, just put it down as them all." You want to help the participants focus as you start narrowing down the problem you want to fix first.

REVENUE

Does solving this problem actually bring in money or help generate it? It is important to discuss what sort of numbers the stakeholders might be looking for here. Devin Birtciel, an engineer in the software industry, once said, "Are these a few dollar ideas or million dollar ideas" to stress the point that while a product could generate revenue, there is a chance it might not be much. There is an amount that has to be initially invested before something might turn a profit, so don't think just in terms of how much it could make but also discuss the budget of resources such as time and money that need to be invested first. Will the business come out even, at a loss, or does the revenue ultimately outweigh the costs? It may seem incredibly straightforward, but as mentioned earlier, if you do not intentionally talk about it, chances are no one will and you want to reduce that chance.

PRODUCTIVITY EFFECTIVENESS

Will this improve the workflow of you yourself, individuals, or systems? Ask these questions:

- Does it enable automation of some sort?

- Does it bring transparency into an area?

- Does it change someone's life in a positive way?

It is important to really sit with these questions and not rush through them for the sake of doing it. Dig in and find out how it improves productivity. Ask the Product Team Members, "Are any of you expecting a change in behavior from a system, team, or specific user?"

REGULATORY AND COMPLIANCE

Is this something that has to be done in order to meet standards? Depending on your industry, products that are mandatory, can cause revulsion. Most companies that are willing to work with both the product mindset mentioned in this book and have something they must comply with or regulate, will tend to be on the later side in terms of timing. So have empathy, try and understand what led the team to get to this point and what already exists to ensure success. In a healthy business that is ahead of the curve or is actively talking with regulators, this is something that usually should be started as soon as you find out about it. Groups not often talked about, but definitely may need to be pulled in, based on your business or resources are the following: legal, architects, HR, and especially security.

AVOIDED COST

Not to be mixed up with Regulatory and Compliance, this is a cost that you and your business might be predicting that can be avoided if the right product is in place. It is important for this to be understood by all Product Team Members, and for anyone with an understanding of financial or social implications if it is not addressed. You might add additional people from legal, architects, HR, and/or security to the

Product Team Members. Keep an open mind and don't count out any potentially affected group as they relate to the issue being avoided.

MARKET FIT

If you get one of these potential products, you have one of the rarer ones and have an opportunity to really do some trailblazing. If this is the category picked, do not be surprised to be running another Scoping session soon because as you find where the product fits, you will also need to find where the value of the product resides.

3.4

Hypothesis

This is the very first time as a team you get to start the creation of the first hypothesis together. You may have learned what a hypothesis is in a science class. It is a defined statement that will be focused around the value of implementing a solution. If the hypothesis does not reflect the value that will be delivered from solving the problem, spark interest or shed light on a purpose of the potential product's existence with those participating, you may need to pivot. It is important that the hypothesis has a clear value that everyone can agree upon.

The recommendation is to use the standard scientific hypothesis. To start, use an IF/THEN statement. *IF, we implement this particular solution, THEN we should expect to see a result.* It is incredible how many products simply do not have a hypothesis as a foundation. Maybe it wasn't ever identified or it once was, but has since lost its value. Constantly ask yourself if you know the hypothesis and ensure that everyone involved knows it as well. With the entire Scoping session, everyone should be able to repeat the information using the same words and nomenclature.

From this point on, meetings should start with the hypothesis of a product and the value it is deriving from being implemented. This hypothesis is the mantra of a product's being. The fastest way to reduce scope creep, which is undefined functionality which has sneaked its way into the original product direction, is to frame conversations about the product around the hypothesis.

This hypothesis is also the statement which should be defaulted to whenever someone asks what a product is. An elevator pitch should be built out of this hypothesis.

ELEVATOR PITCH

The name says it all—an elevator pitch should be so brief, you can share it with someone riding on an elevator. It should be seen as a way to bring anyone up to speed quickly using a few sentences. Having a clear, agreed upon hypothesis which points to the value will help your team effectively share information about the product to others.

3.5

Description

This is an ideal time to have Product Team Members describe from their perspectives, what the product actually does. Usually the individual(s) who created this potential product have the most to say here, but it is important that all involved have a chance in their own words to speak and describe it. Once you have collected all of your feedback, summarize it. Try to keep the description summary between two or three sentences. If you find it difficult to have a highly focused and trimmed description, then the product may be too big, doing too much, or there is a potential misunderstanding of the problem you are trying to solve.

3.6

Deadlines

If you recall in the last chapter, community is something to be sought after. If that's the goal, it's important to identify actions that could threaten the goal. Deadlines are exactly that. Enforcing strict deadlines is one of the fastest ways to lose relationships, team members, and trust.

Deadlines exist whether they want to be realized or not. Now, do you have to work around them? Absolutely. For example, if you are dealing with a budget, you have given yourself a deadline of how much can be spent on solving the problem before running out of money. It could also be related to people or resources. Stay away from enforcing new or creating deadlines yourself if possible, however, you have to be aware of them and get them out in the open and talk about them if they are needed by a particular user, customer, or business stakeholder. Have an honest conversation about why deadlines may be dangerous to a product and team, and lay out how you plan to include those requesting deadlines with updates early and often as value is delivered. Products should be run without them. The reason you are encouraged to shy away from a deadline when possible is because it can validate excuses to cut corners and increase technical debt, which is work that has to be revisited later if not immediately addressed now.

So how do you get around dates if you are running a product?

Alignment with transparency is key. Rarely will you see an email suffice for alignment; rather what works is getting the right individuals in a room and talking clearly about any deadlines ahead. As soon as you stop talking, you are suffocating the product. Communication is the cadence of the product's lungs. Conversation is the air of a product. Without either of these, the product dies.

In the words of an influential Senior Director of Platform Engineers, Clint Hill, "We deliver software, not deadlines, and we deliver software every day." Show off your progress early and often, which in turn will cut out assumptions and build understanding.

HOW TO DEAL WITH PEOPLE WHO INSIST ON HAVING DATES

Navigating this topic is tricky and one of the quickest ways to get someone to say, "Who is this person? Get me someone else!" Chances are they will not hear exactly what they want to hear. Dates can be incredibly toxic to a product and culture if mishandled. When agreeing on a date, make sure that all parties understand three main things: dates can change, humans are not good at estimating, and that forced dates can lead to cutting corners. The desired goal is to deliver your product, not dates.

As a successful PTC, you must ask questions and challenge accordingly in this area. Here are some questions to help navigate people on the team who insist on having dates.

- Is the deadline because of our product or because of a moment or opportunity? If it's because of a moment, what happens to the product after the moment is gone?
- Is the deadline related to physical events in the world? What changes will need to occur to the product after those events pass?
- Is the deadline related to a change in the business that is permanent? What change in the product is related to that change in the business?
- What are examples from the business where a deadline was successfully met? What changes to the product occurred in those examples?

3.7

Business Goals

In order to keep shared understanding among team members as it relates to the business they are working or delivering for, it is important to identify the business goals for the product.

There are two prominent questions which need to be answered: First, should the business invest in solving the problem? Secondly, can any of these goals be measured? Now if you are the business owner, then you should have a lot to say here and can contribute. If you are having trouble finding someone to answer this, try and validate that you are bringing in the person whose pocketbook is tied to solving the presented problem. There needs to be a desire to know where money is going and what is being bought. Ensure that the problem being solved is what the business wants/needs. Make sure to differentiate here between what a need is and what a want is. As mentioned earlier, it is very much possible to build a product that does not bring value.

3.8

Metrics

Metrics are the vital signs of your living and breathing product. Meaningful metrics can confirm that the product and team are moving in the desired direction and providing the expected value. On the other hand, they can also be critical in understanding when the product may not be on pace, if it's not delivering the right functionality, or if there is a need to change directions. With good metrics, vouching for or against something becomes exponentially easier. Metrics enable you not only to fact-check others, but also yourself. Metrics can give you hard data that will expose what is or isn't working within the product.

Do be mindful, however, that metrics can be used inappropriately. For example, a consumer may try to twist the meaning of a metric and map it to the performance of an individual or team, especially implementers, when not receiving expected results. As the PTC, you have the opportunity to utilize metrics as a way to build confidence in each of the Product Team Members. You need to realize that anything that is regularly measured can in turn cause a significant amount of resistance.

TOO MANY METRICS

Oftentimes, you may go into teams and see that not only do they have metrics, but they have far too many of them. A team or individual can be overflowing with data available to them, but can quickly lose sight of what is relevant or actually revealing value. Too many metrics can give false positives or distract from looking at the actual problems at hand. Too many metrics can start to contradict each other, and from contradiction come opinions and from opinion come making your job very hard when verifying the next best desired outcome.

NOT ENOUGH METRICS

Even more common is that there are simply not enough metrics. You may have plenty of metrics to choose from, but are they valuable?

Imagine for a moment that you have spent years of your life preparing for the grandest of road trips. You and a few friends plan on using a vehicle you have all built from scratch. You have stockpiled food, researched the greatest routes to take, and the greatest stops to make to enjoy the finest of foods. You have met extensively with each person who is a part of this journey, and you all understand the mission. After much preparation, you all load up your vehicle and hit the road. You and your crew drive for a mile when suddenly you hit a tree, and in order to keep going, you switch your vehicle to reverse and back into a pit. This is all because you forgot one crucial detail -- windows. Not only that but you didn't notice that you ran out of food, and you have no more gas, but you didn't realize that because you didn't keep track of your commodities and also did not install a fuel gauge. Metrics are like the windows and gauges of this example which show the truth which lies ahead and behind, and shows what you can handle and for how long. Sure you can make it some distance without these metrics, but it is unrealistic, dangerous, and you are risking other people's well-being if ignored.

METRICS THAT ARE JUST RIGHT

The one metric that matters (sometimes called the "OMTM", coined by Alistair Croll in the book *Lean Analytic*) is a good place to begin this ever evolving pursuit of knowledge. This is the one metric which reflects the pulse of your product. A popular example is the airline company, Southwest, which stated at one point to have only one metric that a majority of the business cared about: Are the planes on time? There are many potential benefits to having a single metric like this and working towards that value. It could result in building trust with customers, higher retention, saving money on late fees, etc. A lot can be derived from a single metric, so don't limit them to provide or be translated into only one value. Below are some starting points to help you identify key points about your metrics.

METRICS THAT TIE TO THE BUSINESS

Sometimes a business will need to know more than just the one metric that matters, and usually those other metrics matter to your stakeholders. The key is to ask the stakeholder what they are presenting to their peers, other businesses, or customers and what can be measured to help them best represent the product's direction and value delivered. Try to come up with one, two or three metrics that tie to the business and it's needs.

METRICS THAT TIE TO THE PERFORMANCE

As the PTC, you need to try and find any potential gaps when it comes to delivering the work that has been scoped out. Some go to great lengths and have even built highly prescriptive monitoring frameworks around this idea, but to start you need to err on the side of trusting your team and using these metrics to verify. It is important to trust but verify. Trust they are getting the work done, but use the agreed upon metrics to verify. The goal of this method is not micromanagement. You are simply ensuring that any potential unhealthy areas are brought to the light as soon as possible. As a PTC, you are not managing the implementers, but you are managing the work, and this is very important to understand. If all of a sudden you see a boost in productivity, you may want to figure out what is working, or if you see that productivity is slowing down, you want to find out what to stop or even automate. Here you will want to try and come up with one, two, three, or more metrics which can directly represent the performance tied to the product.

3.9

Engagement Goals

You may have identified the product and the goal, but who will be doing the work? Choose to be intentional and talk about what teams or individuals are going to do to reach the goals, metrics, values and vision that have been discussed and scoped out.

Sometimes you will be leading a product where another individual will be handed the reins as it becomes more developed. Verifying who will be the PTC and when that person will take the lead needs to be discussed beforehand. If you are a consultancy, or are leading a team, sometimes it is more than just the product, but your presence and teaching that are needed as well. Additional training from experts involved may be important, and this is a good place to make those callouts.

3.10

Market

You need to confirm that before you begin moving forward with a solution that you take the time to see what is out there to be utilized to solve the problem and what solutions exist. If this is not discussed, you run the risk of believing the fallacy that it will be cheaper to build it yourself, but in some cases, this is potentially false. With software, there is an option that you may not need to buy anything and that there is open source software that can accomplish what you are wanting to do.

Before stating that you want to build something collectively, consider the following:

1. Do we have the headcount?

2. Once it is built, what does support or availability look like?

3. What work is required for the work to be compliant or secure?

4. Do we have time?

5. Do we have money?

6. Are we able to build this and maintain it with our current capacity?

Sometimes answering the questions above can save you a lot of money, time, and frustration. Just because you have an idea does not mean you are the one that has to build something. While paying for a service can indeed be costly, when compared to the questions above, it may turn out to be less costly. Look for open source communities, vendors, or other services. Just remember that any of these chosen options still need to be maintained.

3.11

Users

Passion and desire can overshadow this section. As a PTC, you need to make sure the users are a topic which is discussed often. There are many companies where a brilliant product is built; however, there are no users. You can build something that is incredible to use and solves problems you can see, but there is still the chance that no one wants to use it. It is a much more common situation than many are willing to admit. Sometimes it may be a stubborn ideator who wants something because of what they thought will be valuable. Other times, something may be built too late or even too early. All who are involved should be held accountable during this phase with identifying who the users are.

To ensure your success in this area, consider the following:

1. Do you have early adopters? (users who will actively work with the PTC during productization)

2. Do you have the beginnings of a plan for the rollout of your product?

3. Are there systems in place to get feedback early and often?

It is easy to believe that there is no user if you're working with a technical tool or automation. While the tool itself isn't the user, those for whom you are automating the work for is, even though they may not have to do the work once it is implemented. You should always seek to identify a user, even if you are writing something for one computer to talk to another computer. If you are unsure of whom your users are, there is nothing wrong with getting away from the desk and building a network of potential users through meetups, friends, and even family to conduct interviews to find out who the user may be. The key here is to get people talking and identifying who can help guide you on whether you are building a product which brings value from a consumer's perspective.

3.12

Technology Platforms, Dependencies, and Integrations

Knowing what tools, services, or other products need to be involved is important for ensuring the Product Team Members are enabled to move forward and execute in an empowered manner. There are many fantastic products that would bring great value but miss their window due to restrictions or limitations to the integrations needed. Here is a real world example about an anonymous company.

A great set of automations around security was ready to be released to the world, saving about five million dollars a year; however, it was lost and the product was ultimately a failure due to one particular dependency that was not willing to collaborate - the actual security team. The security team felt threatened and were brought into the product after it was already built by another team in another department, thus feeling as if they were not trusted and that what was built may not be secure. The product was ultimately scrapped.

What is important to realize here is that it is not all about whether implementing a solution is possible, but also realizing that there may need to be an inclusion of certain people who can be identified early in order to make sure the window of opportunity is not missed in terms of delivering value. Having **Subject Matter Experts (SMEs)** can be crucial in identifying unknowns which come from someone with more experience in a particular area, and may have the ability to contribute to the product in ways the product team members could miss if they were not involved. Otherwise a team may be unnecessarily discovering how to use something which in turn could take a lot of unnecessary time, and even miss that window of opportunity for the product to be delivered.

Check that the systems and software being used have their licenses trued up, and that services are not going to be deprecated. It would be to no one's pleasure that you build a product around the idea of another service only for it to become obsolete or become too expensive to utilize. Just because you have a tool does not mean it is a good fit. Make certain that the services are actively supported and up to date with what you are trying to accomplish. Make certain that documentation is up to date, support is highly available, and even see if there is an active vocal community around the use of such tools.

3.13

Feature List

This breaks down the actual functionality of the product. At this point, the group will start talking a bit more about the high level steps that make up a solution. All of the previous sections should be decently filled out before tackling this, and make certain you have a problem before you start creating a solution.

This section will sometimes be filled to the brim, and other times there will be loads of questions to be answered but be encouraged, and take heart for the rest of this book will help guide you on how to actually create this list based off of feedback, interviews, and discovery. You need to timebox this section, as it will be clearer as you go through the other steps, but you definitely want to start this conversation to ensure that everyone is heading in the right direction in terms of understanding what the product should generally do.

What a feature is can be greatly debated, but the outcome of each feature should foster a focus that acts as an attribute of the product which hopes to solve a smaller problem or enable a certain functionality.

3.14

Anti-Goals

This is where you get to lay down the boundaries of what should be included and what is not included. This is not the opposite of goals, rather an outcome that strives to answer the following: What are some factors you are aware of now that could disrupt or sneak into the scope of the product? There is an endless supply of work that can be done on a product. It can be similar to the popular saying, "A Product is never finished, only abandoned." AntiGoals help keep you focused on when to stop adding to it, not abandon it.

Scope creep, which is product functionality which has not yet been defined or agreed upon as necessary by the product team members, is the silent killer. Make a conscious effort to try and identify areas for potential scope creep so that you can lead the team in a focused and manageable direction.

When asked, this phrasing can tend to be slightly confusing, and the suggestion is to say to not worry so much about following a particular phrasing, but focus on the outcome here that everyone clearly understands what the product will not do or allow.

3.15

Hosting

One detail that can tend to get overlooked due to the excitement of getting to work on a potential product is: "Who will be hosting and maintaining this product if it is implemented?" As much as you may like to think products can be finished when they are delivered, it couldn't be further from the truth. The reality is that some products will require even more work after they are developed, due to adoption, keeping up with systems, and support.

There are also some products you actually build for an entirely separate group of Product Team Members. In this scenario, once a certain stage of the product is implemented, you may hand it over to them, which in this case, you would want to make sure of their expectations and support needs so that the hand off goes smoothly.

3.16

Risks and/or Unknowns

The outcome of this section is to write down the potential risks, what the team is unsure about, and what needs to be mitigated or researched further before starting to actually implement a solution.

What happens in this section is what directly fuels the next part of productization and the next chapter called the Discovery and Framing phase.

RISKS

Discuss and write likely variables which could cause negative impact or inhibit progress of the product and business. Product Team Members have different angles and blindspots, so try and see the risk from their eyes and how it may affect all those involved.

UNKNOWNS

What you want to do now is to bring out the humility of all individuals by discussing what they are uncomfortable with or unsure of in relation to the product. You may face the obstacle of trying to know what others don't even know about themselves. This is not always the best way to approach each person on your team; instead this is where collaboration across the team is crucial. Start the conversation with the Product Team, and identify additional individuals with different experiences and perspectives to help broaden the horizon of thinking.

MITIGATION

It's great to know the risks and unknowns that may hinder the project, but it is important to have a plan in place to manage the risks and unknowns. When they are identified, attach who is responsible to it moving forward so that you instill accountability into seeking out the answers or findings. Call these action items, as you want to ensure action is taken to mitigate them. Putting a name on each risk and unknown helps bring a sense of ownership that is expected to be acted upon in the Discovery and Framing exercise.

SOME SIGNS YOU NEED TO RESCOPE

1. Finding that you are running out of work for the team

   The work being done is starting to look different than what was agreed upon during your Scoping session, the Discovery and Framing phase, and Inception sessions.
   – The above is not necessarily bad. It could be that the users are already using the product for what it was intended to do, but are needing additional functionality.
   – The product not achieving what it set out to do initially by solving something completely different

2. Finding a different product needs to come out of the work that you are doing based on the needs of what the user is asking.

3. Discovering the hypothesis has been proven.

4. Discovering stagnant metrics.

5. Discovering metrics are moving towards another MVP or problem to be solved.

If you wish to see what a completed Scoping session looks like utilizing the categories discussed, reference the completed Scoping session example in the back of the book (Appendix B). Feel free to use it as a template for any ideas and potential products of your own.

4

Discovery and Framing

Discovery and Framing is a phase, typically lasting two to six weeks, where the identified Product Team Members including the PTC will broaden their search to further their understanding of the problems that may be associated with a potential product that was scoped. You want to give the Product Team Members a chance to look past the general limited scope for a set time and with intentional rigor bringing back any of the findings or discoveries to the entire team. With these findings, you collectively choose the highest value problem to solve out of the list of problems discovered, framing it so there is shared understanding among the team.

Once this has been done for the problems, the same needs to happen for the solutions. Test any current theorized solutions and look outside of what has already been proposed to come up with other potential solutions to solve the problem. Then, the team collectively revisits the solutions so that a single one can be chosen and framed in a way that everyone involved can start working on it. The framing of these solutions is the very beginning of establishing an MVP.

PROBLEMS AND SOLUTIONS

This section will help you identify which problems and solutions are worth going after and which are worth ignoring. You can filter and choose based on the Scoping session results related to the product. The Scoping session results generated will act as a filter for what you need to focus on versus what might be a distraction. To know how to begin discovering, start by following up on the action items generated from the Risks and Unknowns section. One of the keys here is to identify and determine what you believe should be chosen to investigate.

This is when you identify the following:

- What problems are you trying to solve? Pick the most valuable one.

- What do people think about those identified problems? Interview your users and Product Team Members.

- What solutions do you have to mitigate or help with the problem? Pick the top one based on the MVP (most valuable problem).

- What do people think about the solution picked? Interview your users and Product Team Members.

WHEN TO HAVE A DISCOVERY AND FRAMING PHASE

This happens after a Scoping session. Ensure that the team involved in Discovery and Framing phase understands at a high level why this potential problem is being tackled. Do not go into an Inception session yet without a Discovery and Framing phase first.

IMPORTANCE OF THE TIMEBOX

This is not a deadline as much as it is a healthy boundary. By giving yourself a set amount of time to go through a Discovery and Framing phase, you are encouraging intentional focus on the process which will allow you to start delivering something of value and learning. This will also help you prevent the product team from building something of little or no value.

A product can have an endless number of features, and with that, it could also have an endless number of problems. The PTC is responsible for guiding the Product Team away from analysis paralysis, where you have so many options that you cannot decide which to tackle first. The reality is you likely won't get it figured out perfectly on your first implementation, and the best way to learn is to get something in front of the user in a timely manner to begin a feedback loop.

OUTCOME OF A DISCOVERY AND FRAMING PHASE

The goal of a Discovery and Framing phase is to define the hypothesis and MVP for the product based on the top problem and the top related solution. Be sure to mock up any trial designs and get user feedback to test if the potential product needs to persevere or pivot around its original scope.

Who:

PTC for the potential product, one or two implementers, one designer, and stakeholder(s).

How long:

Typically two to six weeks.

Approach:

This is dynamic to the product itself, however, a good starting point is showing prototypes and conducting interviews with potential users. If a system or product is already in place, map out what using it looks like, using diagrams and journey maps. Make sure to create a list of problems found and then make a list of solutions to choose from.

Tips:

- As you interview users, keep track of users who are particularly interested as they will be key for quick feedback. These people are called early adopters.

- For more inspiration on different approaches to this step, read The Lean Startup by Eric Reis.

- This is also a great time to start building a community of trusted PTCs who offer collaboration to find approaches in addition to reading and practice.

What a Discovery and Framing Phase is Not:

It is not meant to encourage progress on a problem to be solved without first validating the problem and then having complete team and stakeholder synchronization on the solution.

HOW TO RUN A DISCOVERY AND FRAMING PHASE

Every Discovery and Framing phase will look different. For some, the uncertainty of what a Discovery and Framing phase is may be exciting, and for others, it is nerve-racking. Wherever you find yourself on this spectrum, the key is to inspire the Product Team Members to focus on the problem first, then the solution. Your goal as the PTC in this phase of the productization is to get people to talk to each other and ensure all who are involved are moving in the same direction and have constant shared understanding. Remember, Discover and Frame the problems, then do the same with solutions.

DISCOVERY

Breaking down this diagram, you initially should be going into this step with a list of problems to investigate. Start with the problems, try and find more problems, climb the peak that is related to this problem and get a different outlook at the top. Make an intentional controlled mess with those involved, especially the stakeholders or users. Explore and ask them about the problems they are facing in relation to what you are wanting to solve. Do not be surprised if some of the problems that come up are not on the original list that you have. Sometimes the problem is not obvious due to factors that could not be viewed based on what you were aware of at the time. Constantly keep yourself open to the idea that the problem to solve might be different from what was originally thought. Do not get emotionally attached to a problem just yet.

Some ways to identify problems:

1. Sit down with users and watch them solve a problem.
   – Watch their workflow, ask questions, and identify any additional pain points you might see.

2. Guess, verify and adjust.
   – Here is a helpful example that comes from product leader Josh Kruck. It helps if you can sometimes make educated guesses and verify with just the people and open information on the internet. The example he used was guessing the number of pianos in a given city. One can think of the average number of people who owned pianos, then look up the population of a particular city and do some simple division. When the activity changed to verify, it was found that the guesses were not incredibly far off. Having an educated guess can lead you on the path to verification which in turn can help you adjust goals or understanding on confirmations and conversations rather than just saying "who knows" or working only off of assumptions.
   – Of course be careful here; you want to make sure not to mix opinion with facts. As a PTC, you should not work off of assumptions but verify everything within your reach

3. Map it out.
   – Similar to the first, you can actually map out from left to right or top to bottom what the process of a problem is. Get as detailed as possible. You will tend to find more problems in the entire journey map than you initially anticipated.

4. Interview!

– If you do not have feedback to work off of, go ask for it. There is nothing wrong with just interviewing potential users by going out and asking people their thoughts. Most people won't share their opinion on a topic unless specifically asked.

– Be prepared with questions when you interview the user. Also be prepared to end the interview, as a timely ending is just as important. Users are not expendable, and they need to be treated as such.

– Check what a majority of users want, not just a single user who speaks loudly.

5. Combine and review results.

– If you have done all of the above or more, make sure to start grouping and combining your findings based on themes. The key here is to validate and have data which clearly represents the problems.

FRAMING

Once you have a list of problems, it is time to choose which ones are the most valuable. Revisit the Scoping session - is your initial problem statement the same? If what was previously understood has changed and you have had to move directions, there is nothing wrong with running another Scoping session. This is an example of why it is important to become comfortable with Scoping sessions often.

There is no perfect way to choose which problem has the highest value. It should match or become the business and stakeholder's goals. Ask the question, "Which of these problems can we provide a solution for that will get beneficial feedback and deliver the highest value?"

It isn't always about which is the fastest, or which will make the most money. It can be more complicated, and the key here is to align with the needs of the business and stakeholder. Value is in the eye of the stakeholder - and every other Product Team Member for that matter.

If you want to be successful, focus on the problem at its core; listen and validate before you begin to perform Discovery on solutions.

AUTHOR'S NOTE: Framing can be a deceivingly difficult outcome to achieve due to the number of emotions attached to each problem and solution presented. For example, one of the problems and solutions could be so exciting and new to work on that the entire team will be motivated to jump on it first. The reality is there may be another more valuable problem and solution set which needs to be worked on first but may be perceived as "boring." Make sure to keep emotions, value, and intentions in check while not being distracted by lower value thrills.

DO THE SAME STEPS OF DISCOVERY AND FRAMING FOR THE SOLUTIONS

So you have a list from which you have chosen a top problem, and the Product Team Members are aligned to each of the identified problems. Now you need to work with Product Team Members on what you are going to solve first.

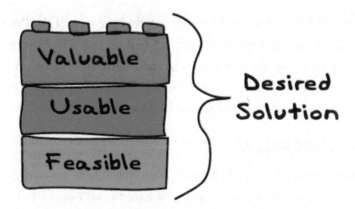

Start solutioning and putting together some proof of concepts to validate. It is important to note that it has taken this long in the productization process to get to the actual solution, and that is for good reason. You do not want to be blinded by what could be built without ensuring there is a problem worth solving.

With the chosen problem that will be solved, try the following:

- Begin to come up with a list of solutions by looking outside of what has been discussed already.

- Walk through the solutions with a user, stakeholder, and designer.

- Watch out for how much "code" could be written here, as it could just be thrown away if another solution is chosen, which can be wasteful and costly due to time.

- Build out wire frames, sketches, and paper prototypes which can be presented in order to observe how a potential user interacts with it.

- Seek which solutions provide the most value and can be built with the resources that can be utilized and ensure the feasibility of the product.

FRAMED HYPOTHESIS AND MVP

Risks and Unknowns should be mitigated to the best of the Product Team Members' ability by this time. You have run a Discovery and Framing phase on the problems and the solutions. Finally, it's time to agree on the hypothesis and create the definition of the MVP as it relates to the top chosen problem and solution.

SUNK COST FALLACY

Just because you have made it to a certain stage in the productization process or product does not mean you have to carry on with it. This is one of the benefits of a Discovery and Framing phase, which is to see the viability of a product. If a product is not valuable, you either need to change the goals, the problem being solved, or even the solution.

Remember, it is possible to build something that is not valuable. Strive to create a culture amongst the Product Team Members where discovering that a product needs to be pivoted, discontinued, or is just not valuable enough anymore is celebrated.

POST-DISCOVERY AND FRAMING PHASE, PRE-INCEPTION

At this point the Product Team Members involved should have a general idea of all that was discussed during the Scoping sessions and the Discovery and Framing phase, but may not have a holistic understanding. Remember that this process can take two to six weeks if needed, and a lot of new information can be introduced. The PTC should be able to piece together the entire product as it specifically relates to each involved Product Team Member, ensuring shared understanding. This is where the Inception session comes in.

PRE-INCEPTION

Before you move onto an Inception session, go over the Discovery and Framing phase results and provide a general question-and-answer forum with the Product Team Members. This step can be incredibly complex and overwhelming if those who participate do not come prepared. It is important to focus on what progress and discoveries have been made, as you want to be sure you have investigated all areas of movement or any areas of potential added value that you are all aware of. Pull up any prototypes, research, findings, videos, and roadmaps. This is when you want to talk about MVPs and the chosen high value problem to solve with all of the Inception participants and all those who make up the Product Team.

There can commonly be a moment in the Inception session when those who were not in the Scoping session or the Discovery and Framing phase come up with questions or problems not found in those activities. The reason this happens often is because during Scoping sessions and the Discovery and Framing phase, you may not have had all the identified implementers or Product Team Members, and most often it's regarding existing solutions with existing problems. As the PTC you want to try and avoid the trap of putting these items into the Parking Lot (introduced in the next section, but it essentially is a tool used that contains topics which are written down and discussed at the end of the Inception session). They can easily get lost or neglected there, and it usually shows up during the development of the product. This particular meeting is meant to mitigate that trap by spending intentional time on newly introduced risks and unknowns.

HOW TO RUN A PRE-INCEPTION SESSION:

Identify the teams that will share. These teams should be the ones with information gathered from Scoping sessions and the Discovery and Framing phase. These teams need to prepare their presentation ahead of time via pre-recorded demos, slides, or other media which allow for streamlined sharing in the larger group setting. Ensure that all get a chance to ask questions and see the data they need to see or are looking for.

5

Inception

This is the time when you get together as a complete Product Team and ensure there is a shared understanding of the MVP, hypothesis, and metrics. You can sort of view this as a Scoping session being expanded, but with many more validated knowns and confidence. The results of a Discovery and Framing phase will be shared and all parties involved will gather around to affirm they have an understanding. The following sections will go through the steps of an Inception session, as well as explain how to create an interactable activity for each step.

WHEN DO YOU HAVE AN INCEPTION SESSION?

This happens after a Discovery and Framing phase when the makeup of the Product Team is identified and the product has been validated to bring value. This is also a great time to introduce a user to all involved, and commence their induction as part of the Product Team Members.

Who:

The PTC for the product itself, The Product Team Members, and any other party involved, e.g., legal or security.

How Long:

Depending on the size of your product and the amount of information you need to cover, the time it takes can vary greatly but general benchmarks will be given on how long a section can take. Generally, it can take anywhere from four to ten hours. When you get started, you will tend to find you need even more time than what was just stated, but that is where you, as the PTC, have to keep everyone focused. If this meeting is not run effectively, you could waste 12+ hours without making any progress. You can show the value and outcome of the Inception session just by keeping it timely. It is not uncommon for experienced teams with clearly defined problems, solutions, and MVPs to complete Inception sessions in four hours. As you become more experienced in facilitating these sessions, you will get a sense of how much more time may be needed as conveyed by the participants' displayed shared understanding.

Tip:

Try using a visual timer that everyone can see. There is no math involved, and everyone can quickly glance and see the time moving and represented.

Outcome of an Inception Session:

Go over the hypothesis and solution the Product Team has agreed to implement, while aligning how its value and progress will be measured in a highly interactive meeting. This is also the official kickoff for the mapping of the work that needs to be done to actually implement the MVP.

What an Inception Session is Not:

It is not meant to be a time to come up with a solution or hypothesis. This should have been extensively discussed and agreed upon during the Discovery and Framing phase.

APPROACH, SUPPLIES, AND SETUP

Invest in an environment that can be highly collaborative and make space for a whiteboard where all attendees can collaborate and write notes, whether this be a digital whiteboard or an office whiteboard. Check that people are in an area with a stable internet connection, and all should have webcams on and ready to go. As the PTC, be sure to take screenshots of the process and additional notes for reference later. Everyone involved needs to be heard clearly and be in an environment that does not present many distractions. If possible, provide lunch for those involved.

5.1

Individual Introductions (5 minutes)

Go around the room and have all state what role they play in the Product Team Members. If you ever get a response that suggests the member doesn't understand the reason he/she is part of the meeting, dig deeper and check that each person understands the critical role he/she plays in this Inception session. If you find that someone does not bring value being there, kindly let that person know that four to ten hours will be returned by your releasing him/her; and most will be happy about that. As discussed earlier, watch the room carefully for those who are speaking the loudest. This is important because some personalities you can start to identify before the meeting begins by observing how everyone interacts with each other. You are not expected to be some expert of psychology, but do your best to intentionally read the emotions and personae of a room as a facilitator.

Encourage the attendees to ask questions, but be sure to have those involved answer the following questions:

- How are you specifically involved in the project now?

- How will you be involved in the future?

- What are you hoping to get from this meeting?

5.2

What is an Inception Session? (5 minutes)

The PTC explains to everyone that the idea of this gathering is to instill shared understanding before implementing the actual solution and hypothesis. There must also be a shared agreement to the metrics that will be measuring success. Go over what steps this product has gone through via Scoping and Discovery and Framing before this meeting as well as a very quick summary of each activity to come in this Inception session. One of the outcomes of this step is to explain how information related to the product is understood and shared consistently. This should resemble an elevator pitch that everyone can share with anyone who asks about the product. This establishes consistency with the state and direction of a product.

5.3

Introducing the Parking Lot (2 minutes)

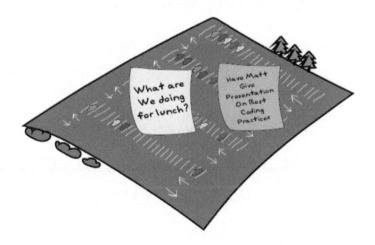

When running longer meetings, a lot of perspectives will be shared. It is important to listen and filter that the topics discussed are relevant. A visualization to help your team is called "The Parking Lot".

As these irrelevant topics come up, take note and put them where everyone can see it; this is to show that you are not just brushing it off. Once you have written down in this way, put it on a virtual sticky note and put it in a section called the Parking Lot and explain that after the Inception session or in the subsequent days you will address it.

When you start doing Inception sessions with a group that is familiar with all the steps, they will sometimes want to jump ahead, which shows good motive but can easily derail the meeting. Try to display a copy of the agenda and have them add a statement to that section on their own that they can reference when the time comes. Not all distractions are parking lot items, but the timing might not be right. Above all else, make sure you make time to actually address the parking lot items, as it builds trust and shows that you value the words the participants felt concerned enough with sharing.

PARKING LOT SETUP

Draw a digital box on a collaborative white board. Make sure there is plenty of room for digital sticky notes to be put within it.

5.4

Product Name and Elevator Pitch
(10-20 minutes)

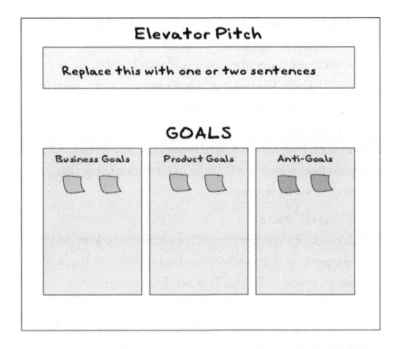

Similar to Scoping sessions, this step checks that everyone agrees with what the product will be referenced. From this point on, if you hear older names or a name that does not represent what was agreed upon, kindly correct the person. At this point, you are creating the mental and verbal branding for this product, and you want everyone consistent on the matter.

The elevator pitch may vary from what was originally scoped to new information discovered during the Discovery and Framing phase. Do not just rely on the previous Scoping session. Try and describe what it does in one or two sentences. This elevator pitch also acts as a lightweight-guardrail for the rest of the meeting and can help determine whether a topic may need to go to the Parking Lot or not.

ACTIVITIES FOR PRODUCT NAME AND ELEVATOR PITCH

Make sure everyone is starting to head in the right direction in one of two ways:

1. Collective Wordsmithing
   Have participants just start talking and pick out words that everyone is nodding their heads to or that seem to really stick out. For instance when someone uses a word to describe something, you may hear someone say "Oh, that is good! Make sure it includes that." Write out the one or two sentences, have everyone read it out loud, and iterate. After several iterations you will begin to have something that resonates with everyone.

2. The "Reveal" Method
   This can lead to great success depending on the knowledge of the product that everyone has leading into the Inception. Have everyone, individually, write down one to two sentences describing what they think the product does. After each person presents, pick and choose among them and frankenstein together the elevator pitch.

5.5

Goals, and Anti-Goals (45 minutes)

It is now time to collectively focus on each of the goals and anti-goals. This should be done one at a time, with the intent of answering why this product matters to the business, what value it brings, and what the focus of the product will be with this particular iteration.

Business Goals (15 minutes)

In this section you want to focus on what goals the business and stakeholders hope to accomplish by funding and supporting this product.

Some examples of a business goal would be:

- Time to market "improved" when a new feature is implemented.

- Ensure you can scale the product's dependencies up or down as the users fluctuate.

- Reduce the cost of ownership.

Products Goals (15 minutes)

What does this product do and hope to accomplish or offer?

Some examples of a product goal would be:

- A repeatable and consistent service you can offer to users via mobile interface.

- Enable implementers to be self-sufficient.

- A fully automated experience.

Anti-Goals (15 minutes)

What does this product not do? Does the business understand what this product will not solve? An anti-goal is not simply the opposite of what was just defined; rather it is something that is specifically detrimental to the goals.

Some examples of anti-goals would be:

- Requires users to submit a ticket when the product is unavailable.
- Requires 24-hour human support.

ACTIVITY FOR GOALS

Set a timer for five minutes of silence when no one is allowed to collaborate or talk. Very rarely do you let this happen; you typically want people to talk. However, in this moment, it helps prevent bias and brings out one's own thoughts. Focus on one section at a time and have everyone write on virtual sticky notes. Once they have theirs completed, have them put the notes up on the whiteboard. For example, if you focus on just the business goal, first have everyone write down their sticky notes in their own area and then post them after five minutes in the business goal section. After they are posted, then have each person speak to the goals they wrote. If you find that many are similar, feel free to group sticky notes or even stack them, but make sure that the one that represents the grouping is easily viewable, agreed upon, and on top.

Once this is done, move on to the next section which in this case would be the product goals and do the same thing.

Once you have all of your business goals and product goals written by everyone, then distribute three votes for each section, in this case it would be three for the business goals and three for the products goals. All persons can then put those votes on the sticky notes they believe are the most valuable or important. They can put all three on one sticky note or two on a sticky note and two on the other, etc. This voting should be done in silence as those who are typically boisterous can tend to sell their ideas and sticky notes. Once this is done for the business goals, then proceed to do it for the product goals. After both sections have been voted on, move the most voted goals to the top (Focus on one to four goals) in each section. These are especially important because they will help flesh out metrics later on.

Next is the anti-goal section for which there is no voting. All persons will put up their sticky notes and then proceed to present to the rest of the participants the ones they came up with. The facilitator ensures each one is talked about and groups any similar ones together after checking with each note's creator. This section is especially important as it represents the group's ability to grasp signs of scope creep. Don't just talk about the anti-goal and call it a day. Discuss and write down the mitigation for each goal as well. You want to check that everyone understands how the anti-goal will be handled if it were to come up again.

Take a Break (10 minutes)

This is a good time for people to stand up, take part in bio-breaks, check email, or take a quick call if needed. Make sure to state when everyone should be back, ready to work, and make it clear that you have everyone's best interest in mind to keep this moving along.

5.6

Risks and Action Items (1 hour)

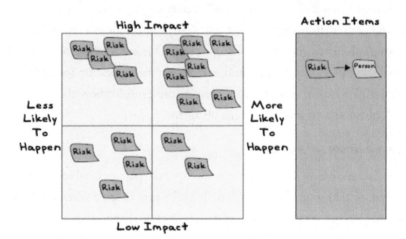

Risks have a bit of a setup and explanation but will ultimately yield insight to some of the most dangerous blockers or inhibitors. Explain to your team that this exercise will help identify any risks which could be dangerous to the success of the business, user, or product if they continue to exist.

A risk should be viewed as something unrelated to the product that could impact the product team, e.g., high-turnover, a pandemic, slow hiring, budget. If you have made it to this step, a risk should not prevent the product from being built or work from being started; rather, it is something that needs to be monitored to avoid it from turning into an unexpected disruption.

A risk in this exercise shouldn't necessarily be tied to a goal or anti-goal. Anti-goals and goals relate to the product itself, while a risk's focus should relate to variables outside of the product goals and anti-goals. These terms can easily be confused, so verify that your team has clarity about each of these definitions.

ACTIVITIES FOR RISKS

Setup (10 minutes)

Firstly, draw a picture (see illustration) with four squares representing a grid with the words "high impact" and "low impact" on the top and bottom respectively, and "less likely to happen" and "more likely to happen" on the left and right respectively. You also want to create a space for action items to be placed.

Have each person write a minimum of three risks but a maximum of ten on individual sticky notes. After they are all written, have each person take his/her top 3 risks they feel are the most relevant and put them in an area of their own. Many times you will find that there will be duplicates or that the remainder of sticky notes they could have put up have been covered by one of the other Product Team Members.

Placement (10 minutes)

Have everyone place their top three sticky notes on the grid. Explain that the X axis represents the likelihood of a risk to happen. The negative X-axis represents a risk that is not likely to occur, while the positive X-axis represents a risk that is very likely to occur.

Explain that the Y-axis represents the impact if a risk were to be fulfilled. The negative Y-axis represents a risk that would have little to no impact on the business, goals or people involved, while the positive Y-axis represents a detrimental risk.

AUTHOR'S NOTE: Be ready to redraw the grid *(see illustration).* Most people will put their sticky notes in the top right due to a healthy domain bias each of them bring to the table and the scenarios they experience daily. For example, you will find a security team will most likely put risks around ensuring whatever is built is safe and free from backdoors for hackers. In contrast, designers may not have security practices at the forefront of their mind but want to ensure that whatever is built is usable by the consumer in a way that will bring a sense of accomplishment. If you find that a majority of sticky notes reside in the top right, feel free to draw the grid again with that cluster of sticky notes as a way of reducing noise in that quadrant and bringing attention to the sticky notes that are at the top right. This also forces the teams to be honest about what risk is legitimate and not simply their pet concern. If someone mentions a sticky note needs to be in the top right after you redraw the grid, feel free to move it there to bring some ease of mind.

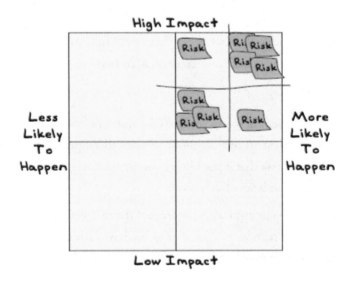

Grouping (5 minutes)

Pick a few participating individuals to help group and organize some of the posted sticky notes. If two sticky notes are placed on the board that are similar, before grouping them, take note of where they are placed and meet halfway for their place of residence. Group and label risks to find patterns, themes, or concerns which may need to be addressed.

Discussion (10 minutes)

Discuss each group of sticky notes, focusing mainly on those which are likely to happen and have a high impact (those at the top right of the grid). Go through each risk and have the persons who wrote them present what the risk is from their perspective and have others in the room address the concern. If the concern continues to persist and cannot be fully mitigated, then move onto the action item phase.

Action Items (10 minutes)

You want to make sure to write down what the risk is and then assign a person to the risk to mitigate it or lead the mitigation effort. These risks should be brought up daily in a ceremony (more on those soon) which meets until resolved after the Inception session.

Tip: If a person cannot shake the feeling of talking about a risk not in his/ her top 3, bring it up and discuss it. Remember that empathy is one of the most important qualities of a PTC.

Take a Break (10 minutes)

5.7

Persona Mapping (1 hour)

The goal of this exercise is to map out, at a high level, the different people with whom you will be dealing with during the implementation of the hypothesis (more on that in the next section). This exercise gives a better understanding of the mindset you may need to adopt when talking with other teams or users. This is one of the most empathy-inducing exercises that is done as part of the Inception session. This is also where you can begin to learn the value of User Experience (UX) which you are encouraged to research further. UX is not only a trade, but an artform that plays a critical role in many product teams. It dives into technology and how humans interact with it in a way that is beneficial for product teams to understand.

ACTIVITY FOR PERSONA MAPPING

First establish the number of Persona Mappings you will be doing. Do this by posing the question, "From our current knowledge with what groups will this product need to interface with in order to be successful?" You may get answers like, "The implementers (application engineers)", "The user (a kid)", "Dependent team (the network team)", "The stakeholders", etc.

For each group you have identified, create a four-squared template (see illustration) with the words "Demographic", "Challenges", "Thoughts", and "Workflow". Next, break out into teams of two to three people to fill out and represent the Persona Mapping. Assign to the team the relevant role being filled out. For example, if a team is filling out the template for the stakeholder, then there should be at least one stakeholder present on that team. Once the teams are established, get to work by filling out the quadrants and presenting.

Filling Out (15 minutes)

Each of the teams will work on filling out each section to the best of their knowledge. Try not to do too much guess work here.

Demographic

The focus of this section is to get to know your group and how you may need to approach them. Be thoughtful about the level of knowledge of everyone on your team or in this group. For example, if someone is not technical, it wouldn't be wise to spend time showing them what the implemented code looks like.

Some examples of demographic are: the age range of the people in this group, where they are located or their geolocation, their experience related to the problem, their technical ability, etc.

Challenges

What struggles, frustrations, or desires does the particular person want to mitigate or desire a solution for? Make a list of findings that have been confirmed during Discovery and Framing; this should tend to follow what the elevator pitch hopes to accomplish from earlier, or at least fall into a general theme as the elevator pitch.

Thoughts

This is the time to write down what the particular group is thinking at the moment, such as, "If I have to manually export data from this spreadsheet one more time, I may have to start looking for another job" or "There has to be a better way". Be intentional about capturing their feelings and thought processes.

Workflow

Using journey maps, flowcharts, or anything in between, chart what their current work looks like. If you have extra time, you can also focus on what you may want it to look like, but use this sparingly. This will help identify what their day-to-day looks like, and can even bring up additional problems that may need to be addressed or anti-goals which need to be discussed.

Presentation (2-3 minutes each)

Each team will then pick a representative to go through each of the quadrants in front of everyone and speak to any of the sticky notes. If possible, have the person who is part of that persona group speak to the persona that was just mapped out.

After each person has gone, move onto the apex of what you have all been working towards since you first came together.

Take a Break (10 minutes)

As mentioned earlier, ensure all participants have a chance to clear their head, get some water, or take care of any distractions that may have surfaced since the last break.

5.8

Hypothesis (15+ minutes)

ACTIVITY FOR ESTABLISHING THE HYPOTHESIS

When writing and reviewing the hypothesis, make sure your elevator pitch, business goals and product goals are in sight of everyone. They should be referenced and reflected on while writing the hypothesis. The hypothesis should have already been defined during the Discovery and Framing phase; however, during an Inception session, some verbiage may need to be adjusted.

The hypothesis is the driving force of all the work done so far. This is the statement which you will bring up daily and weekly. This is what defines whether a conversation may need to happen or may be a distraction. If done right, your hypothesis will be directly tied to the MVP of your product. There are many different methods for writing hypotheses, but the one suggested is the "If/Then" format as mentioned in the Scoping chapter.

Generally you want to stay away from multiple hypotheses as it can turn into a very bloated product. If there are multiple, ask the team, "When reading all of the hypotheses presented do you still think of one product?" If the answer is no, you should collectively remove the conflicting hypotheses. The hypothesis should map to the already defined business and product goals.

5.9

Metrics (15+ minutes)

ACTIVITY FOR DEFINING METRICS

One to Three Metrics That Matter

Work together collectively to come up with one to three metrics which will represent the progress, success, or health of the hypothesis you just came up with. These are the metrics that you will be sharing daily and weekly with your product team, or whenever you have a meeting with a stakeholder. Use them liberally. If you don't have any metrics, then you have no way of validating assumptions. A good PTC does not work off of assumptions. With these metrics, you can collectively ensure that you are heading in the desired direction. Keep in mind that the same metric may need to be translated differently depending on who is consuming it. For example, software engineers may be interested in how often their codebase is down so they can track how often they have to work off-hours to try and bring it back up. However, a stakeholder may need that same number to be mapped to the length of time the product is down which prevents users from accessing the service in turn halting transactions to occur.

Go back to the metrics section in the Scoping chapter as it goes into detail about why they are so important there. As a reminder, metrics should instill confidence, not cause resistance.

5.10

Story Mapping (1-2 hours)

This is a high level overview of what story mapping is, from an implementation point of view, but theory and supplemental knowledge is needed and highly encouraged.

AUTHOR'S NOTE: This section is not a substitution for reading the book User Story Mapping by Jeff Patton. He introduces what collaborative shared understanding and storytelling is all about. It is highly supplemental and can create opportunities for your own product journey by creating more meaningful conversations while structuring work and goals into a story that others could understand and contribute towards. The book you're reading would not exist if it weren't for Patton's work. It is highly recommended that you read his book to get as much as you can out of this next section.

EPICS, FEATURES, AND STORIES

These terms may be new to your team, and that's okay! They are meant to be guidelines and give shared vocabulary to aspects of the process. At the end of the day, the outcome you are after is organizing work in an understandable and digestible way. These three terms may help you get there.

Epic

Epics are what make up hypotheses. An epic contains either a single feature or multiple features. Epics can be used as a high level way of organizing work. In many product management tools, you can correlate a label to an epic which you can filter/search for stories and features by. An epic should represent a larger functionality or suite of functionalities which are available when the feature(s) it contains are delivered.

Feature

A feature is a functionality or category of work that shares common ground. A feature has multiple stories that make up its existence. Utilize features to organize the day-to-day work that will be done and usually reference it within the title of a story. Features should be used as a way of filtering into what category a story falls. A feature should seek to deliver something which is noticeable or usable when the attached stories are delivered.

Story

A story is the smallest amount of deliverable work which validates the hypothesis. Multiple stories typically make up a feature. In the Inception session, only focus on the title of a story and do not flesh it out fully yet. A story should not be dependent on other stories if it can be helped. To understand this fully, read the next chapter (Story Theory) to see what a story should look like after the session is finished.

EXAMPLE OF STORY MAPPING APPLIED

The illustration below, which was heavily inspired by Patton's work, displays a story mapping from left to right. As the PTC, try to use a non-technical example of story mapping so that anyone can more easily follow along.

This may seem very simple, and that is for a good reason. Use this example when explaining story mapping to those who may not have read about the process or are unfamiliar.

In the following, it first starts with mapping the high level, which is the epic level, called "Morning Routine". This epic would be attached to a hypothesis which states, "If I have a morning routine, then I can get to work on time while not being as stretched for time."

If a morning routine is implemented then the hypothesis can begin to be validated. What makes up a morning routine, one might ask? A few elements include hygiene, food, and movement out of the house. What makes up each of those features can be broken down further. It's easy to think that once you have those implemented , you are finished. Well, you might have someone say, "I don't eat breakfast", "I work from home", or "I take a long time to get dressed". This is why collaborative story mapping is valuable. Remember your goals and hypothesis that were defined earlier, and begin to seek that the story map being created echoes the work needed to implement the MVP. Always be driving and steering the conversations around what was just established in this Inception session.

This story map is read left to right, and top to bottom. What needs to happen first should be at the top left.

ACTIVITY FOR STORY MAPPING

Have multiple colored sticky notes and ensure they are tied to a category (epics, features, or stories). Make sure not just one person is writing them and that everyone in the room is contributing. Start with five to ten minutes of silent story mapping in which all participating are writing out their sticky notes and putting them on the whiteboard. During this time, anyone can rearrange, make notes on other people's stickies and silently collaborate. Once the time is up, it is time to talk through the work being presented. This can be very noisy, and you need to check that everyone is taking turns speaking and representing their sticky notes. Every sticky note should be discussed and confirmed. The sticky notes should have just enough on them to represent the work that needs to be implemented. Ensure that each one is understood by those who will be working on it.

5.11

Recap (10 minutes)

ACTIVITY FOR INCEPTION SESSION RESULT RECAP

Walk through the story map that was just created while all of the
Inception session information is visible. Everyone should listen intently,
and as the PTC, ensure that the story map falls within the bounds
of the hypothesis, metrics, and goals. If any part is not within those
bounds, identify how it got in and why it may not be needed any more
for validation of the MVP.

5.12

Gathering Feedback to Improve the Inception Session (15 minutes)

ACTIVITY FOR GATHERING FEEDBACK AND PARKING LOT

After the Inception session, it is important to spend time on the topic of the session itself while focusing lightly on the product. This will most likely not be your last Inception session, so you want to make sure you are adapting it to the business and team's needs.

For now just do the "what went well," "what could be improved," and "what went poorly" style as explained in the Weekly Ceremonies chapter. Set a timer and have everyone put at least one item on the board. These items can help you create constructive feedback.

Over time, you will begin to craft an Inception session from what is discussed here which is finely tuned to the business and Product Team Members needs.

5.13

Post Inception Session

FROM INCEPTION SESSION TO ACTIONABLE WORK

It is time to work with the implementation leader to begin writing full-fledged stories. To store and track these stories, start by choosing a technology that enables you to manage a backlog and easily move stories around. Move all stories that were mapped during the Inception session into a list and start to wordsmith. Fill them out with the appropriate data so they can be discussed, picked up, worked on, and opened up with clarity by the appropriate Product Team Members. For a good starting point on how to write effective stories, read the next chapter on Story Theory.

PART III
Story Theory

This section intends to equip you with a customizable story framework which can be adjusted for conversations, direction, and work by writing them down in a format which can be referenced by your Product Team Members.

6

Stories

Stories exist to catalog shared understanding of work that needs to be done by having them written down in an organized and referenceable fashion. Each story should be written by the PTC to ensure the list of stories is carefully organized in a way that is focused and leads to the validation of the hypothesis and implementation of the MVP. Ultimately, a story acts as a reminder to have a conversation or acts as a place where a previous conversation can be referenced.

When utilizing stories, it is important that you write them in a way that the information contained within them is easily digestible by the implementers, the PTC, and anyone else who may come across them. Here is a framework for writing a story, including examples of a good story and bad story, similar to what you may see in the tech field.

6.1

Story Framework

Title:

The feature this story is tied to, and a very short description.

Description:

AS A [USER]
I WANT [FUNCTIONALITY]
SO THAT [REASON/VALUE]

Write this area from the perspective of the user so that it explains the functionality and reason as it relates to them.

Sometimes the user is a system, and that is okay. Simply have the system be the user. Have the developer themselves act as the requestor or the "user". For example, if an automation needs to be done that only the developer or implementer would be aware of, the description would start like, "As a product-developer I want.."

Avoid attaching multiple descriptions in order to keep stories small so that they can be delivered and the results can be measured quickly. If you notice any instance of the word "and" in the description, double check that it does not need to be broken down further.

Acceptance Criteria:

GIVEN [General setup and context]
WHEN [Something is performed]
THEN [Expected result]

These criteria are what the PTC and Product Team Members will use to test whether a story has been implemented according to the understanding discussed during the ceremonies and throughout the week.

A trap some fall into is being tempted to have a larger acceptance criteria in order to compensate for multiple things being implemented or tested. If the conversation becomes, "*...then* X will happen, *and* Y will happen, *and* Z should happen", you may need to reevaluate. It may be a sign that a story is too big if a list of things need to occur in order for the story to be accepted.

Artifact(s):

Provide any conversations, feedback, wireframes, design drafts, architecture, attachments, to have readily available. Any implementer of the product should be able to open a story after it is discussed and get to work without having to hunt down the information from others.

6.2

Good Story

The following is an example of a well written story which can equip you if you have all the information needed to fill it out. Additionally, this story sets up a scoped conversation, which leads to shared direction and understanding.

Title:

Metric Dashboard – The stakeholder wants to view the uptime metrics for the week.

Description:

AS A Stakeholder
I WANT to be able to view the uptime metrics on a dashboard for a product
SO THAT I can determine whether we are losing any money due to downtime

Acceptance Criteria:

GIVEN I visit the dashboard related to a product
WHEN I click on "View all metrics"
THEN I should see that the uptime metrics

Artifact:

"All of the needed designs are attached and downloadable as a .jpg of the format that this story needs to follow."

What Makes This a Good Story:

- What is being requested is easily understood at a high level, based on the title alone. This is important for someone who needs to constantly keep track of all stories in an organized list.

- The user is established, which is important information when demonstrations or conversations about the implemented work needs to happen. It also instills empathy into what is being built because, at the end of the day, you are working with humans.

- Acceptance is in complete correlation with the users' needs.

- The resources are readily available and all in one place.

- It is simple and easy to grasp.

6.3

Bad Story

The following utilizes the same example as above but displays what would be considered a bad story.

Title:

Uptime metric

Description:

Need to be able to see the product metric

Acceptance Criteria:

Go to page and see product uptime metric on dashboard and click on a button to generate report

Artifact:

Go ask Andrew or Janice for the mockup

What Makes This a Bad Story:

- The title could mean many things—the opportunity for misunderstanding is high.

- It's not clear how the user is affected.

- It's highly subjective about when the story actually ends.

- The user's wants are not established.

- The acceptance criteria conveys that this may be multiple stories.

- None of the resources or artifacts needed are readily available, preventing the story from being ready to be worked on.

6.4

Story Variants

Sometimes you will find that certain work needs to be chosen or put at the top of the list to keep the product in a healthy state. Chores and bugs are simply stories, but they were unexpectedly introduced to your team.

Chore:

- A type of story you were not planning to work on.
- A part of the product that people don't see, but without it, there would not be a product.

Bug:

- Revisiting an old story which should be treated as a new story having to reevaluate something that didn't work how you thought it would.

Ultimately you want to create a space where work is effectively communicated and shared understanding is written out for all to reference. Having this collective of shared understanding and stories will ultimately lead to successful ceremonies which will be covered in the next chapter.

Next up is how to carry forth a daily and weekly execution of stories that have been created. This will help equip you with ceremonies to be used as tools to help align all Product Team Members involved.

COMMONLY ASKED QUESTION:

Where is the section on pointing stories?

First it's important to understand where pointing actually comes from. Pointing came from the idea of wanting to provide two things:

1. A mechanism in which a stakeholder could tell how a team is progressing.

2. It was a way for consultancies and businesses to try and estimate their costs.

Though on paper this might seem to provide some value, it actually doesn't measure the value of the product in the slightest. If you pull back the curtain, all pointing exists just to provide "managerial comfort" and is not tied to what is considered a product metric.

Be warned that pointing can lead to burnout, mistrust, or contain a lot of false positives that do not encourage a healthy work/life balance. In order for a team to consistently hit their amount of work estimated, they may begin to cut corners to attempt to achieve a certain quota of points by a team in a given iteration.

There is however, a way in which pointing can work well! This shift in thinking requires points to be viewed not as a means to estimate when something will get done, but rather as a means of assuring and gauging shared understanding. Pointing can be used as a quick way to check the confidence of the team based on their experience, or knowledge on a topic in relation to the current product hypothesis. Keep it simple, unanimous, agreeable, and ensure that it is easy to understand and use. If executed well, it can lead to the desired outcome—shared understanding. If it is not all of those things, then you either need to revisit if points are needed at all or simplify it further.

PART IV

Ceremonies

The following ceremonies provide the Product Team Members with arranged and curated outcomes that will drive communication during the execution of stories. Using the following ceremonies, you can build out what daily and weekly expectations will look like for the PTC and Product Team Members. Ceremonies will help move the implementation of the MVP along, and should help build momentum while you work collectively as a Product Team to validate the hypothesis. Each ceremony will cover the expected outcome, how often it should be utilized, and which of the Product Team Members are involved.

Keep this question at the front of your mind as you run a ceremony: *Do the Product Team Members have what they need, do they understand the product, and are they ready to work?*

AUTHOR'S NOTE: One of the concepts that is purposefully avoided here is calling a ceremony by a stylized name as it relates to a specific Agile or delivery style. The focus here is the *outcome*. What a ceremony is called is not important—the information you seek, which conversations are encouraged, and shared understanding are important. Lifetimes can be wasted arguing what to call a ceremony. Instead, be intentional to center the focus and conversation around what values are being sought after within ceremonies.

7

Ceremony Setup

Let's first cover the bases of what a ceremony is. It's important that you approach every single ceremony with the understanding that you are dealing with a human's most valuable resource—time. Not only are you facilitating these ceremonies, but you are also ensuring they end on time or earlier if needed. There needs to be a constant respect of scope, and every member who is responsible to contribute needs to be present and active. You are a PTC because people can trust you not only with this work, but trust that you will respect them, too. Since ceremonies are about achieving an outcome, if there is no outcome, there is no ceremony. Communicate the objective and provide an agenda of any ceremonies early and often to remind participants why they happen. Do note though, that not every interaction with Product Team Members needs to be a ceremony. A rule for when you should email or use another form of communication outside of a ceremony is when sharing information does not require the contribution of another party.

You may be wondering who should be involved in these ceremonies. Your expertise, previous interviews, and constant building of relationships should help answer this question. If a person is not contributing to solving the problem, that person does not need to be there. Each individual in the ceremony needs to have something unique and valuable to offer.

Constantly watch the room to assess how often and how much certain Product Team Members speak. If possible, have a shared screen on which others can interact or share. When participants constantly see their thoughts being written down and polished by others in the room, shared understanding can more easily be established. This can be highly effective in ceremonies and can help add a visual aid to what is being discussed for those who process information visually.

DESTROYING SILOS WITH THE ENCOURAGEMENT OF ENGAGEMENT

When dealing with each Product Team Member, ensure that the shared understanding is not just happening between yourself and a few other members. This can create something called *knowledge silos*. Knowledge silos are when SMEs (Subject Matter Experts) begin to answer all of the questions or become the only persons who can answer or implement something. This is a dangerous place to be because it leaves the team vulnerable if the SME suddenly becomes unavailable. It is important that you help prevent what is called the "hit by a bus" conundrum. Let's say there was a specific Product Team Member who was the only one who knew what was happening behind the curtain of the product. If that person was suddenly hit by a bus, had medical leave, or some other sudden thing happened to them, you would immediately be left with a gap which no one else may have been prepared to fill. Naturally, this causes the momentum of the product to be lost, or unnecessarily vulnerable. It is incredibly risky to rely on one or two members, or SMEs. Equip the team, including yourself, so that anyone can confidently speak to the hypothesis and technical aspects as it relates to their contributing area.

CEREMONY CADENCE

You need to ensure that as the following ceremonies become part of your daily and weekly routine that they continue to stay focused. After a while, they may feel like they are losing their intended value or focus if the hypothesis and value is not brought up often. As a team gets more comfortable with your product, it is important to remind them that the comfort they feel comes from communication and performing the ceremonies well. Understanding the importance of ceremonies is so critical that some companies even have a dedicated job to leading effective communication through ceremonies outside of the PTCs duties.

KEEP CEREMONIES TIMELY

Ensure the PTC runs them so that all participants are aware of the time. If one of the ceremonies takes ten minutes and you have six team members, that is nearly an hour of collective time a day dedicated to that ceremony. As the PTC, it is your job to make sure the right people are in these ceremonies and that they are run as effectively as possible in order to honor everyone's time.

COMMONLY ASKED QUESTIONS:

What kind of Agile is best?

The best form of Agile is the one that both delivers value and ensures shared understanding daily. Since outcomes are the goal, it doesn't quite matter what kind of Agile-style you should or should not do. If you really would prefer to discuss this, here are some general tips. *The Agile Manifesto* is an extremely helpful tool. If you have to choose, look for something that puts people first and leads to constant conversations instead of just a process. While this resource is robust, there's much to learn about Agile from different kinds of books, blogs, and salespeople—find a resource that works for you! You are encouraged to avoid the pitfall of only doing something one way for the rest of your life or the product's life. An Agile style that is dogmatic will lead to missing out on valuable iterations of your product's evolution. Be flexible and open-minded to the ever-changing knowledge available to you!

The Agile Manifesto is one of the foundations of this book, specifically around collaboration with individuals and interactions, and responding to change.

For more information about *The Agile Manifesto,* visit agilemanifesto.org to get a baseline understanding.

XP vs. Scrum vs. Kanban vs. some other style?

There are so many different ways to tackle your week(s) in terms of communicating with the teams involved. Try each of them out to find the one that works best for you. Some might focus on touching base once a week, while others might work on it every other week. Whatever it is for your team, be willing to test them out! That might sound time consuming, but just because you learn it, does not mean you have to use it. There are so many certifications one can get for each of these styles, which is great for people who want to dive deeper. However, beware of the Sunk Cost Fallacy. This fallacy can trick you into thinking that though you may be an expert on a way of working and have spent a lot of time learning something, you must use it because it is the right one. You may actually find that it doesn't jibe well with a certain implementation, and that is okay! The only "right way" is the one which empowers people to do the work that needs to be done while communication is encouraged. Remember that people have limited headspace, so you need to be in constant communication. Make sure you do not instill a one and done style of communication, where you only talk about something once.

Ultimately you will find that picking just one is a potential trap. Picking the parts that bring the most value from each as they relate to your product's space is the best approach.

How often do you perform the ceremonies?

As often as you can to ensure the Product Team Members have what they need, understand the product, and are ready to work. To start, try the daily and weekly ceremonies covered in this book and iterate on the cadence from there. It is not meant to be a hard and fast rule, but displays a sense of urgency to validate that what is being created, curated, and maintained is valuable and does not allow stale information to form. You want to close the gaps for assumptions and not give hysteria a chance to get a grip on anyone's perception. Having ceremonies often can help prevent this.

8

Daily Ceremonies

This section will cover both daily ceremonies and weekly ceremonies. Use this framework to help create the best cadence for your team. The title of each ceremony is the outcome which should be sought after.

8.1

Daily Shared Understanding

Ensure shared understanding of the entire team daily, by verifying each individual on the team can say:

"I have what I need."

"I understand the product."

"I am ready to work."

Remember, these three statements are the mantras which carry these ceremonies.

Who:

The PTC, the entire technical/implementation team, and any additional Product Team Members.

How long:

10 minutes or less

Facilitator:

The PTC

Key Points of Focus:

- Do all team members have what they need to get their work done?

- Do all team members understand the product at a level where they can see how their contribution is part of the iteration?

- Does each team member understand the current product hypothesis?

- Are there any blockers or inhibitors?
  – What conversations can be had outside of this ceremony to mitigate them.

- What has been done since the last time we all met?

- What will your focus be today?
  – This checks that work is not duplicated. There are few things more painful than work being delivered twice within the same team by two different Product Team Members.

- What action items generated from other ceremonies that relate to the team's health and happiness need to be addressed?

- Remind everyone of any upcoming ceremonies and the current scope of the product.
  – Over time teams can often take on more and more in terms of scope creep. It is up to you to validate that what is being talked about is relevant to the current hypothesis and goals.

What the Application of this Ceremony Looks Like:

One of the ways this can be accomplished is by having a voice and video gathering to focus on each Product Team Member individually. There should be no notifications, phones, or distractions. Have each person involved answer the three questions:

"Do I have what I need?"

"Do I understand the product?"

"Am I ready to work?"

As the PTC, remember that people are incredibly forgetful, so repeating the vision, direction, and what is being worked on needs to be stated often.

8.2

Shared Understanding at End of Day or When Handing Over Work (Optional)

Keep in mind that out of all the ceremonies discussed, this is the one which may be optional; however, this could also be the difference between successful communication and chaos when dealing with a product that has a lot of moving pieces.

You run these the same way you would a ceremony in which you seek daily understanding as mentioned above, but may do it at the end of the work day or when handing it over to another team whose day is just starting. This can be helpful when dealing with a team globally, for example. It can also be critical when releasing a new feature, or when bracing the team for a quick change that suddenly came up. You may even utilize these meetings as a temporary way to communicate often, to ensure all Product Team Members are aligned a few times a day as needed.

8.3

Acceptance of Delivered Stories That Need to Be Validated

You want to set up a time when stories delivered from your Product Team Members can be reviewed as soon as possible so that they can be accepted. The "who" is an important part of this process and, pragmatically, it may not even be the entire team at one time. This is the time for the team member to show off their work with clearly defined rigor. For instance, try to use this ceremony as an exercise to validate that the outcome can be shown or described to someone else on the team who is not a part of building it.

If a story is accepted, then you can receive feedback quicker from the intended user it was built for. If it is not accepted and returned back to the implementer quickly, then it is still fresh in the Product Team Members' minds and they can address any of the potential shortcomings or changes that need to occur in order for you to accept it.

Who:

The PTC and the implentor of the work.

How long:

However long is needed to fully understand what was delivered and ensure it is understood.

Facilitator:

The PTC

What the Application of this Ceremony Looks Like:

Sit down with the one who delivered the story and review the acceptance criteria of the story. You want to make sure that any new information discovered during the implementation of the story is written down and applied to any other stories that may benefit or be affected. Guide the deliverer of the story to answer any questions you might have around how it was implemented and validate that it works in the way expected from the requestor or user.

9

Weekly Ceremonies

These are ceremonies that should be held once a week rather than daily due to the time-consuming nature that includes gathering more data. If the frequency of your ceremonies isn't at least once a week, the potential of gray areas increases and communication can be hindered. Just like with the daily ceremonies the title of each ceremony is the outcome which should be sought after.

9.1

Shared Understanding Between the Implementation Lead and PTC

The goal of this is to reveal the collective implementers work by talking with their nominated implementation lead and align it with the direction of the product.

If you are a non-technical PTC, this is a great time to further your own understanding by discussing details with the technical lead for the presentation to the Product Team Members. Being transparent about what areas you do not understand is not a sign of weakness or ignorance. It represents a desired understanding that the product is being built and delivered in a manner that a more general and broad audience accepts.

Who:

The PTC, the lead implementer, designer

How long:

One hour or less

Facilitator:

PTC

Key Points of Focus:

- Add any necessary stories that have been discovered as they relate to the current hypothesis and MVP.

- Remove any unnecessary stories to deliver the MVP or hypothesis.

- Ensure stories are fleshed out and ready to be worked on by any of the implementers on the Product Team (see chapter three).

- Choose which stories should be worked on first based on feedback, user needs, and highest value that can be achieved quickly, if possible.

- Set up the list of stories in a way that all of the implementers can pull from the top, or choose what is considered the next most valuable deliverable.

- Attach any designs or artifacts to stories that need referenceable context.

What the Application of this Ceremony Looks Like:

The PTC will share his/her screen and each of the stories in a list which contains all of the stories related to the MVP. Collectively work with the lead implementer to pull in any additional stories or remove those that are no longer relevant to the product's scope. Once all the stories have been discussed, the ceremony is over, and you are ready to discuss with the team collectively. As mentioned, this also may be a time when you will work with the implementation lead to further understand any product decisions made by the Product Team Members.

9.2

Shared Understanding Between the Implementation Lead and the Entire Product Team

The goal is to equip the implementation team and Product Team Members with agreed upon work that can be delivered until you all meet again in this forum. Remember to focus only on work that is directly tied to the hypothesis and MVP as defined for the current product.

Who:

The PTC, the entire implementation team, the designer

How long:

One hour or less

Facilitator:

PTC

Key Points of Focus:

- Focus on where you just came from since the last time you had this ceremony and where you are going.

- Keep the ceremony short and focused

- If you find there are not enough stories to be worked on, be transparent about it and work with the technical lead to translate the user's needs and stakeholder's asks into stories related to the current hypothesis. Reschedule this ceremony later in the day or week if needed.

Create a shared understanding for the stories in the list yet to be worked on.

- Start by looking at any stories in progress. This gets everyone synced quickly about where the product is.

- Work your way from the top of the list and go through every story. These should have already been chosen based on value and should begin to tell a collective story when next to each other.

- Check that stories are small. This enables stories to be delivered daily.

- Ensure everyone on the team understands the stories to avoid knowledge silos.

- This is the place where editing or validating existing details of each story occurs. You can always reference chapter three to validate if a story is fleshed out properly.

Check that there are enough stories for the team during the week.

- This should be treated as a daily tally of work. Avoid trying to timebox or put deadlines on the work being asked whenever possible.

- This comes down to focus and not trying to plan out the entire product before you have validated plausibility.

- There will always be features to implement, but it is up to you to decide which ones will be worked on next.

What the Application of this Ceremony Looks Like:

The PTC will share his/her screen and open up the tool used to keep the list of stories. The one implementing the stories will go through the stories that are ready to work on. The team should bring up any additional details they feel need to be added, break down large stories into smaller ones, or ask for further clarity.

Here are two useful questions to ask your team:

"Do you all understand the story as written?"

"Are you all confident that this story is ready to be worked on?"

9.3

Team Health and Product Health Check-In

It is important to create a safe and controlled environment to discuss what went well and what did not. Once these items have been discussed, you can begin to create action items to handle anything you wish to continue or cease.

Oftentimes, unhappy teammates make bad products. Creating a safe space where people feel comfortable expressing themselves will help draw out any problems in a more constructive manner than someone simply complaining. This is the place to clear the air, help people vent, and allow the team to help individuals having trouble.

Who:

PTC, Product Team Members, implementation team, designer

How Long:

One hour or less

Facilitator:

Rotate who runs this ceremony. Different facilitators may pick up on different emotions or see angles that another might be blind to.

As the facilitator, encourage everyone to speak. Those who tend to be more reserved may not say anything unless given an opportunity or asked.

Key Points of Focus:

This is not a complaining session, but a forum to collaborate on how to strategize to be successful. This is like a huddle at the end of a week. Great product victories happen by forming strategies... not complaining!

Many things can be covered in this ceremony. Everything from the working environment, communication between roles, and technical decisions should be discussed.

Be intentional to make this ceremony fun and productive. It is a great time for the team to connect. Bring snacks and enjoy this time together as a team.

If the action items generated from this ceremony have no consistent follow through, it can quickly turn into a platform for complaining. The actionable results need to be taken care of quickly to establish healthier and happier people and patterns.

What the Application of this Ceremony Looks Like:

Only two styles of this ceremony are provided for you below. Feel free to research further into other variations.

STYLE ONE:

What is Working Well, What Needs to Be Improved, What Needs to Stop

Create the following four sections (see illustration on next page):

- "What went well?"
- "What could be improved?"
- "What went poorly?"
- "Action items"

Have all present go around the room to discuss one thing that is on their minds as it relates to the three sections. Be sure they place their thoughts in the respective categories. After each person has done this once, open it up for everyone to do freely. Action items should be created for anything that needs improvement or simply went poorly. These action items should act as reminders for someone to take action to help mitigate an issue from continuing. Bring up actions items daily until they are resolved.

| What went well? | What could be improved? | What went poorly? | Action items |

STYLE TWO:

Pirate Ship Check-In

The general idea for this visualization is to provide a more robust selection of categories to place your sticky notes. These sections include:

What moves us forward?

- What habits or patterns are driving the Product Team Members in the desired direction?

What are our goals?

- What are the goals of the product, hypothesis, and MVP and how do you check to see whether they have shifted since it was last discussed?

What holds us back?

- What patterns or setbacks need to be improved upon?

What are potential dangers for us?

- What areas could be dangerous to the team or the product if left unchecked?

Have everyone put up sticky notes of areas to be called out or processed. These can be related to the team, the product, the business or any other scope of work. Talk through each of these points, create action items that are tied to an individual or team, and ensure these action items are followed up on.

9.4

Demo the Work That Has Been Delivered, and Establish Understanding or Gain Feedback

The goal here is to show what is currently being built by the team, the status of the current hypothesis being tested, and any metrics attached to the product. Show any new functionality and try to receive feedback. This will help you lead the product towards the valued direction. It may be advantageous to provide a Question-and-Answer session with the PTC and Product Team Members as they may have demos of their own they need to prepare.

Who:

PTC, Anyone else who could receive value from seeing progress of the product

How long:

The actual demo should be two to ten minutes.

The Question-and-Answer portion can vary—take as long as you need to ensure shared understanding.

What the Application of this Ceremony Looks Like:

All parties involved gather around the PTC and are updated on the following:

1. Current hypothesis

2. Metrics

3. Journey of the product so far

4. Achievements, progress, and work in flight

5. Q&A

Consider pre-recording your demo. This will ensure you end promptly and have time for Q&A. A pre-recorded demo can also be shared with people who were not there, shows the product without distractions, and keeps the discussion on topic.

PART V

Conclusion & Further Thoughts

WHAT'S NEXT?

After going through all the previous chapters, you are now equipped with the knowledge to productize and run the product using daily and weekly ceremonies. Take what you've learned and begin practicing. You won't be perfect off the bat, but expecting failures and extracting learnings from them is the best way to learn. If you are not yet in the industry, or are looking to transition into a full-time position, check out the quick synopsis and some general advice for how to break into the industry below.

Realize that this is just the beginning, not the end all-be-all. When reading this book, be reminded that this is not the only way to run a product. These are proven methods that have had incredible success within companies as large as 100,000+ employees as well as a single person.

EXPLORE THE WORLD OF PRODUCT

If you find that variants are working well for you and your team, keep doing them. This book provides outcomes to pursue which enable better organization and conversations. Everything written about has been proven and works for many existing PTCs and products. What is highly encouraged, though, is whatever is chosen, that everyone you interact with understands the terms and practices you use. Don't waste time trying to be perfect; instead seek for consistency, empathy, and a shared understanding.

Do what works best with your involved Product Team Members remembering everything you do should be an iterative process which you should be constantly trying to improve. Methodological dogmatism can be the very killer of product innovation.

If you've made it this far, you're ready to start working on valuable products and seeking feedback as a Product Team Coach!

AN ASK FROM THE AUTHOR

Please leave a review on Amazon or from whatever platform you got this book. Your feedback is appreciated, as due diligence will be had with any valuable input. After all, it has been user feedback and experience that has shaped each chapter of this book.

SUGGESTED ADDITIONAL READINGS

User Story Mapping by Jeff Patton

Lean Startup by Eric Ries

Proximity Principle by Ken Coleman

PART VI

Breaking Into the Industry

For those not in an industry with a product presence or product people:

Take heart, as some of the best PTCs out in the world did not start until much later in their lives or have experienced other industries. Contrary to popular belief, you do not need a degree to get into this industry. In fact, many PTCs who do have a degree do not have it in something related to productization. They simply use their wisdom from experience to apply it to productization. The biggest skill to invest in is your ability to represent yourself and others in a highly empathetic and confident way.

Those already near a product industry:

For those of you who are already in the industry where PTCs are present, you may be a few steps ahead. First of all, you don't have to convince anyone near you that they may need product practices or product people since they are already familiar them. If you do have to do some convincing, you now have a book you can use to validate your claim. Secondly, you most likely already know a few people you can begin to network with or a manager who can help give you the opportunity to be a PTC.

For those of who are the business owner or stakeholder looking to implement this:

You now have the knowledge to arm yourself or others as PTCs. Encourage those who are passionate about shared understanding and are highly empathetic to begin running productization and ceremonies.

FOUR RECOMMENDED STEPS:

1. **Research and practice.**
   Don't stop seeking information to make yourself a more valuable asset for your team. The books mentioned earlier are great resources with which to start. Additionally, look at product roles posted by businesses and have them inspire and drive your research to areas you may be less knowledgeable about.

2. **Make a portfolio.**

   Keep track of the products you have managed, especially
   their metrics and value. This can be done by using a simple
   website, blog, or by capturing in your resume. If you do
   not have products yet, show off areas that are related to the
   skills required of a PTC, and leverage those as experience.

3. **Meet people in the industry.**

   Attend local or online meetups and be sure to ask
   questions while building a network. Try to meet those
   more experienced than you. If you can, communicate
   your aspirations to those around you, especially to those
   who are in the industry; they may end up referring to or
   thinking about you when they need something.

4. **Create a positive presentation of yourself**

   Market, promote, and present this presentation in every
   space you can. If you do not get the first job you are going
   after, do not give up! Well educated and empathetic PTCs
   are needed, and in high demand.

HIGH LEVEL INTERVIEW PREPARATION

1. Investigate what a business does and what its missions
   and values are.

2. Learn what the business is looking for in the job
   description. Choose two or three of these expectations
   and tell the interviewer how you plan on delivering value
   to those directly when you start.

3. Go into further detail about how your past research,
   attributes, experiences, studies, skills, and achievements
   reflect that you are the person needed on the team.

Resume

For some, preparing a resume can be daunting. However, taking the
time to intentionally craft a professional resume will set you up for

success. John Marty, a career strategist and financial freedom advocate, has some great tips to help this task seem less daunting.

1. Keep your resume to one page, no more. Let every single word on the resume carry value. Write out all you think is needed, then try to "cut it in half" and see if it still exhibits all the points you are trying to convey. The idea of cutting all that is written in half comes from Joshua Collier, an expert in leadership and leadership development.

2. Metrics which display value are worthwhile. Try to display any metrics and confirmed hypotheses which are of significant value. For example, "I implemented <product> which resulted in <result>."

3. Avoid acronyms. Even if it is common in the industry, just spell it out.

4. Ensure that your online presence reflects what you are stating. The online presence may cause those hiring to learn more about you.

5. Find someone you can speak to in person or over the phone to present to. The human element of this step is to help get around all systems which may be in place since a lot of current jobs have filters and automated systems which sort through applications without a human being ever actually laying eyes on your submission.

How to Communicate Your Value as a PTC:

This template can be used to help others understand the value of this role:

"Based on the research that I have done on the position you are hiring for and the missions you are wanting to accomplish, I believe I am the person you need for the role.

In a similar role to this one, I have accomplished <insert any achievements>, and those achievements enabled me to deliver <related value to the above achievements>.

Secondly, after extensively researching your company more, I respect that you value <company value>, which I also value. My current colleagues can attest to this.

Finally, for the last <number of months or years>, I have loved the work I have done. I read any books I can get my hands on, follow certain product figureheads, attend certain meetups, and I see myself in this industry for the foreseeable future. I am looking for a team that not only pushes me, but allows me to sharpen myself and those around me."

Appendix A

Glossary

Action Items: Responsibilities given to an individual to allow for follow up which achieves a result.

Anti-Goal: What a product will not solve, is not in scope for the product and a way to discuss and write what may be detrimental to a product's goals.

Blocker: Something that inhibits progress or communication.

Build-Measure-Learn: A concept and high-level framework utilized in Lean development.

Ceremonies: A cadenced gathering of the Product Team Members to achieve an agreed upon outcome.

Demo: A time in which you show off the functionality of a product.

Discovery and Framing: The second part of the productization process when the identified Product Team Members, including the PTC, create a list of problems and solutions to choose from based on the needs of the process.

Epic: A collection of features which thematically implement functionality.

Feature: A slice of work with a shared goal, usually used as a label and stated in the title of a story.

Feature List: Related functionality which makes up a larger part of a product.

Hosting: The dwelling place of the product physically and/or digitally.

Hypothesis: A product validation used to prove whether assumptions are true or false based on the information that is available now and in the future.

Inception: A productization ceremony where all involved Product Team Members gather to ensure shared understanding of the MVP, hypothesis, and metrics.

Iterate: Taking learnings from metrics, conversations, and discovered information and adjusting an approach accordingly.

Knowledge Silos: Information which is contained and only accessible within a select group of individuals.

Metrics: One of the product's vitals which reflects and instills confidence, direction, and/or value.

Minimum Valuable Product (MVP): The smallest deliverable which brings value. It is used to check whether a product is heading in the right direction and enable the feedback process to begin with delivered work.

- The "V" is redefined in this book to mean "Value" instead of "Viable".

Persevere: Continue to implement based on the feedback you are receiving.

Pivot: To change the direction or functionality.

Problem: A pain point which needs to be solved and the typical starting place of a product.

Product: Something that will be delivered, measured, and iterated on.

Product Team Coach (PTC): The person who is the center of communication of a product, taking care of the product throughout its ideation, productization, implementation, and feedback phases.

Product Team Members: Sometimes referred to as the collective. This group consists of the stakeholders, implementers, designers, users, PTC, and any other hands-on role related to the product.

Productization: The process of taking an idea and turning it into a product.

Project: Something which may have an end state or desired result which may not need to be improved upon or continued once implemented.

Scope Creep: Additional requests or functionality which do not fall within the current working hypothesis the product is scoped to.

Scoping: The first step in the productization process. It's a conversation that ensures shared understanding and calibration with the direction of a potential product with all parties involved.

Solution: A direction which leads towards the solving of a problem as it relates to a product.

Stakeholder: The individuals who want to know whether a product being built is worth their time and money.

Stories: Small, deliverable functionality reminders to have conversation, or can act as a reference to a previous conversation.

Story Mapping: A versatile tool to enable participants to organize, align, and prioritize a series of thoughts and conversations; popularized by the book *User Story Mapping* by Jeff Patton.

Subject Matter Expert (SME): An individual who has a deep understanding on a particular topic.

User Experience (UX): The experience around how a user interacts with a product, team and business.

Appendix B

Scoping Worksheet

EXAMPLE SCOPING SESSION DOCUMENT

Name

- Unavailable System Ticket Updater

Product Team Members/Requestor

- Anthony – PTC
- Gabe – Stakeholder
- Devin, Jessica, Temo, David – Implementers
- Jen – Designer

Value Category (Pick one)

1. Revenue
2. Productivity Effectiveness

3. Regulatory and Compliance

4. Avoided Cost

5. Market Fit, Potential for one of the above.

Hypothesis

- If we implement automated tickets, which communicate when our systems go down, then we will save the business $X million while reducing any downtime when breaches could occur, freeing up any implementers to focus on the problem.

Description (Tell us about the problem we are trying to solve.)

- Currently developers are being pulled away from their daily work in order to find out why the company's systems are going down. This gap in understanding makes the business more vulnerable, and pulls teams away from their focus of delivering new value.

Deadlines (Dates we need to be aware of.)

- We have a big meeting with Mrs. Jackson, and she is expecting a demo by Q4.

- We are moving to another system and need to ensure that it happens after January 12, 20XX.

Business Goals (Why should the business invest in solving this? Can any of these goals be measured?)

- Reduce cost of maintenance. We could measure this by capturing the time it takes someone to perform the task manually versus how long it takes the automated program to do the same.

- Reduce the cost of developers being pulled from their normal work.

Metrics (How do we measure the success of this product?)

- Every time an incident happens, it takes an average of ten hours from eight different people. Maybe we could measure how much time and money has been saved when it is automated.

Engagement Goals (What output or services do you need from the Product Team Members?)

- Security needs to be involved so we don't overlook any details when automating updates.

Product Goals (What should this product accomplish?)

- Automate ticket creation.
- Automate the process of resolving and documenting the cause of an outage.
- Insight into how an issue is being handled via notifications on laptops and phones.

Market (What could be bought or configured to solve this problem?)

- CrazyMonkey is a product used by other companies that we may want to look into.
- LightsOut is an open source tool which could solve this problem.

Users (Who will the users of this product be?)

- The security developers
- Auditors
- On-call engineers

Technology Platforms, Dependencies, and Integrations (What will we need to interface with when making a solution?)

- Must be deployed on a SeegadaMeeka's server.
- Business's incident software for ticket creation.
- The security team needs to ensure that any communication

with the ticketing tool is secure

Feature List (What should this product specifically do?)

- Create tickets

- Ticket closure

- Notification system to let impacted teams know when something is resolved

Anti-Goals (What does this not do?)

- This does not manage outages dealing with sensitive client information.

- This is not a website and is not intended to be broadly interacted with.

Hosting (Will we be hosting this for you or will you be hosting this?)

- Once built, we will host it and maintain it.

Risks and Unknowns (Anything you do not know or that would prevent us from moving forward.)

- We do not yet know the new platform we are going to be moving on to—the PTC will dig in further.

- We still need approval from John Billamson before moving forward—the stakeholder will ensure the securing of the budget for this.

- Not sure if our current ticketing system allows for third party development—implementers will look into this further via documentation and conversations with the ticket systems developers

Bibliography and References

Cohn, M. (2015). *User Stories Applied for Agile Software Development.* Addison-Wesley.

Croll, A., & Yoskovitz, B. (2014). *Lean Analytics.* Universidad Internacional de La Rioja, S.A. (UNIR).

Kolmodin, M. (n.d.). *The Speedboat Retrospective | Dandy People.* Retrieved August 1, 2015 from https://dandypeople.com/blog/the-speedboat-retrospective-free-download-of-poster/

North, D. (2006, September 20). *Introducing BDD.* Dan North & Associates Ltd. Retrieved August 1, 2015, from https://dannorth.net/whats-in-a-story/

Patton, J., Fowler, M., Cooper, A., & Cagan, M. (2014). *User Story Mapping.* O'Reilly.

Ries, E. (2019). *The Lean Startup: How Constant Innovation Creates Radically Successful Businesses.* Penguin Business.

Citations

"We deliver software":

(C. Hill, personal communication, October, 2021).

"Few dollar idea or million dollar ideas" – Devin:

(D. Birtciel, personal communication, 2019).

Southwest Airlines Example:

(J. Patton, personal communication, May 2017).

How to break into the industry section:

(J. Marty, personal communication, April, 2021).

"Cut in Half":

(J. Collier, personal communication, May, 2015).

Guessing Pianos:

(J. Kruck, personal communication, May, 2016).

Discovery and Framing influence:

(Pivotal Labs, personal training, August 2015).

Special Thanks

Jessica Collier

My wonderful wife and I have four children together (Maybe more kids to come, only God knows). I was able to interview countless people and write this book nearly every night, and she supported me every step of the way. My goal was to write this book before my thirties, and with her help, this happened. I would not have made it into this industry without her selfless support. I could easily fill this book with the support she provided, but I will leave that for her and me outside of these pages. Jessica, I love you dearly.

My Kids

I am gonna take a small break from writing. Let's play games, go eat, and create some more adventures together!

My Dad

You read this book in its rawest form. You didn't just read it; you took notes on every line, and even inspired the name "Product Team Coach". You dared spend an immense amount of time pouring over the book just as soon as it was drafted and spent countless hours commenting and challenging its beginnings. Thank you so much. I am honored that the title reflects your inspiration.

My Mom

I love you. Thanks for raising me and teaching me all while being an incredible mom who has motivated me to work hard, love God, and love others.

Granny and Papaw

Your immense amount of love and support through every season helped shape me into who I am today. I love you both.

Joshua Collier

Love you Josh—thank you for helping me make decisions when at a fork, connecting me with some incredible talent and friends which elevated the information in this book and how it is presented, encouraging an audiobook version, and even shopping for over 5 hours for the right wardrobe. Your support has been cherished and appreciated. Thanks for making memories and securing some solid brother time.

Isaac Collier

Through the many late nights of writing, and keeping me company during the entire writing and publishing process, thank you so much for your love and support even when you were going to the beach on Tuesdays for your picture paintings which help inspire the art in this book.

Hope Collier

Thank you for being the best fashionista extraordinaire I know.

Greg and Renee Carlson

Thank you so much for the immense amount of support and for raising an amazing daughter.

Jared and Riley Carlson

Thank you both for opening up your home in my early years which built a foundation for where I am now.

Clint Hill

Clint, you have an eloquent way with words, and I am so grateful to have you as an ally with every sentence of this book. Your push for precise communication helped bolster the words of this book with confidence, clarity, and the setting of a new standard.

Matt Eland

Thank you for always taking the time to be a supporter, whether it be by "hype chickens" or by being a dear friend who strives for a certain quality which I cannot find elsewhere. I am truly blessed to know you.

Matt Curry

Thank you so much for giving me the opportunity to not just not get into this craft but to get world class training. You always challenged me to strive for more. You believed and invested in my early years and continue to do so. I cannot thank you enough for your mentorship and friendship. You are very dear to me.

Josh Kruk

Thank you, Josh, for bringing structure to some of my productization thoughts. You helped me organize them in a way that I could scale myself and first displayed what it meant to teach in a larger setting.

Jeff Patton

We have only talked a few times, but every time we did, it had an enormous impact on how I perceive the creativity which goes into the craft of productization. Thank you for writing your book, which in turn inspired me to write this.

Megan Zein

Megan, thank you for advocating for me during the early days of software and introducing me to many of the people I am thanking in the book. You were a start to this journey, and I want you to know you had a big impact on ensuring I started off strong.

Bobby Wilson

Thank you for your friendship and instruction in engineering.

Zac Klabunde

Thank you for your incredible friendship and opening up your home during engineering school.

Wesley Merkel
Thanks, Wesley, for being an absolute chief and good friend.

Jake "Scrambo Slammy" Marwil
Thank you for being a great friend both personally and professionally.

Beth Barela
Your early support did wonders for my family, and it kickstarted the journey to want more.

Shayleen Smith
From a lump of coal to a diamond, thank you for taking on the challenge of the first pass of polishing the written aspect of this book.

Mrs Gugeler AKA Mama G
Beginning in high school and through my adulthood, your love, legacy, and support is the only reason I am able to write an entire book.

Seth Farmer
I never thought it would be possible to look this good

Lindsey Baker Allred
Thank you so much for applying your keen eye throughout this entire book, and bringing it to the next level.

Books:
User Story Mapping by Jeff Patton
The Lean Startup by Eric Ries

Made in the USA
Coppell, TX
30 April 2022

77211051R00090